The author's farce; and The pleasures of the town. As acted at the theatre in the Hay-Market. Written by Scriblerus Secundus.

Henry Fielding

Eighteenth Century
Collections Online
Print Editions

Gale ECCO Print Editions

Relive history with *Eighteenth Century Collections Online*, now available in print for the independent historian and collector. This series includes the most significant English-language and foreign-language works printed in Great Britain during the eighteenth century, and is organized in seven different subject areas including literature and language; medicine, science, and technology; and religion and philosophy. The collection also includes thousands of important works from the Americas.

The eighteenth century has been called "The Age of Enlightenment." It was a period of rapid advance in print culture and publishing, in world exploration, and in the rapid growth of science and technology – all of which had a profound impact on the political and cultural landscape. At the end of the century the American Revolution, French Revolution and Industrial Revolution, perhaps three of the most significant events in modern history, set in motion developments that eventually dominated world political, economic, and social life.

In a groundbreaking effort, Gale initiated a revolution of its own: digitization of epic proportions to preserve these invaluable works in the largest online archive of its kind. Contributions from major world libraries constitute over 175,000 original printed works. Scanned images of the actual pages, rather than transcriptions, recreate the works *as they first appeared.*

Now for the first time, these high-quality digital scans of original works are available via print-on-demand, making them readily accessible to libraries, students, independent scholars, and readers of all ages.

For our initial release we have created seven robust collections to form one the world's most comprehensive catalogs of 18th century works.

Initial Gale ECCO Print Editions collections include:

History and Geography
Rich in titles on English life and social history, this collection spans the world as it was known to eighteenth-century historians and explorers. Titles include a wealth of travel accounts and diaries, histories of nations from throughout the world, and maps and charts of a world that was still being discovered. Students of the War of American Independence will find fascinating accounts from the British side of conflict.

Social Science

Delve into what it was like to live during the eighteenth century by reading the first-hand accounts of everyday people, including city dwellers and farmers, businessmen and bankers, artisans and merchants, artists and their patrons, politicians and their constituents. Original texts make the American, French, and Industrial revolutions vividly contemporary.

Medicine, Science and Technology

Medical theory and practice of the 1700s developed rapidly, as is evidenced by the extensive collection, which includes descriptions of diseases, their conditions, and treatments. Books on science and technology, agriculture, military technology, natural philosophy, even cookbooks, are all contained here.

Literature and Language

Western literary study flows out of eighteenth-century works by Alexander Pope, Daniel Defoe, Henry Fielding, Frances Burney, Denis Diderot, Johann Gottfried Herder, Johann Wolfgang von Goethe, and others. Experience the birth of the modern novel, or compare the development of language using dictionaries and grammar discourses.

Religion and Philosophy

The Age of Enlightenment profoundly enriched religious and philosophical understanding and continues to influence present-day thinking. Works collected here include masterpieces by David Hume, Immanuel Kant, and Jean-Jacques Rousseau, as well as religious sermons and moral debates on the issues of the day, such as the slave trade. The Age of Reason saw conflict between Protestantism and Catholicism transformed into one between faith and logic -- a debate that continues in the twenty-first century.

Law and Reference

This collection reveals the history of English common law and Empire law in a vastly changing world of British expansion. Dominating the legal field is the *Commentaries of the Law of England* by Sir William Blackstone, which first appeared in 1765. Reference works such as almanacs and catalogues continue to educate us by revealing the day-to-day workings of society.

Fine Arts

The eighteenth-century fascination with Greek and Roman antiquity followed the systematic excavation of the ruins at Pompeii and Herculaneum in southern Italy; and after 1750 a neoclassical style dominated all artistic fields. The titles here trace developments in mostly English-language works on painting, sculpture, architecture, music, theater, and other disciplines. Instructional works on musical instruments, catalogs of art objects, comic operas, and more are also included.

The BiblioLife Network

This project was made possible in part by the BiblioLife Network (BLN), a project aimed at addressing some of the huge challenges facing book preservationists around the world. The BLN includes libraries, library networks, archives, subject matter experts, online communities and library service providers. We believe every book ever published should be available as a high-quality print reproduction; printed on-demand anywhere in the world. This insures the ongoing accessibility of the content and helps generate sustainable revenue for the libraries and organizations that work to preserve these important materials.

The following book is in the "public domain" and represents an authentic reproduction of the text as printed by the original publisher. While we have attempted to accurately maintain the integrity of the original work, there are sometimes problems with the original work or the micro-film from which the books were digitized. This can result in minor errors in reproduction. Possible imperfections include missing and blurred pages, poor pictures, markings and other reproduction issues beyond our control. Because this work is culturally important, we have made it available as part of our commitment to protecting, preserving, and promoting the world's literature.

GUIDE TO FOLD-OUTS MAPS and OVERSIZED IMAGES

The book you are reading was digitized from microfilm captured over the past thirty to forty years. Years after the creation of the original microfilm, the book was converted to digital files and made available in an online database.

In an online database, page images do not need to conform to the size restrictions found in a printed book. When converting these images back into a printed bound book, the page sizes are standardized in ways that maintain the detail of the original. For large images, such as fold-out maps, the original page image is split into two or more pages

Guidelines used to determine how to split the page image follows:

• Some images are split vertically; large images require vertical and horizontal splits.
• For horizontal splits, the content is split left to right.
• For vertical splits, the content is split from top to bottom.
• For both vertical and horizontal splits, the image is processed from top left to bottom right.

THE

AUTHOR's FARCE;

AND THE

Pleasures of the Town.

As Acted at the

THEATRE in the *Hay-Market.*

Written by *Scriblerus Secundus.*

———*Quis iniquæ*
Tam patiens urbis, tam ferreus, ut teneat se?
Juv. Sat. 1.

LONDON:

Printed for J. ROBERTS, in *Warwick-Lane.*

MDCCXXX, [Price 1 s. 6 d.]

PROLOGUE.

Spoken by Mr. *JONES.*

TOO long the *Tragick Muse hath aw'd the Stage,*
   And frightned Wives and Children with her Rage.
Too long Drawcansir *roars,* Parthenope *weeps,*
While ev'ry Lady cries, and Critick sleeps.
With Ghosts, Rapes, Murders, tender Hearts they wound,
Or else, like Thunder, terrifie with Sound.
When the skill'd Actress to her weeping Eyes,
With artful Sigh, the Handkerchief applies,
How-griev'd each Sympathizing Nymph appears?
And Box and Gallery both melt in Tears.
Or, when in Armour of Corinthian *Brass,*
Heroick Actor stares you in the Face,
And cries aloud with Emphasis that's fit, on
Liberty, Freedom, Liberty *and* Briton ;
While frowning, gaping for Applause he stands,
What generous Briton *can refuse his Hands?*
Like the tame Animals design'd for Show,
You have your Cues to clap, as they to bowe?
Taught to commend, your Judgments have no Share;
By Chance you guess aright, by Chance you err.

   But Handkerchiefs and Britain *laid aside,*
To-Night we mean to laugh, and not to chide.

In

PROLOGUE.

In Days of Yore, when Fools were held in Fashion,
Tho' now, alas! all banish'd from the Nation,
A merry Jester had reform'd his Lord,
Who wou'd have scorn'd the sterner Stoick's Word.

Bred in Democritus his laughing Schools,
Our Author flies sad Heraclitus' Rules:
No Tears, no Terror plead in his Behalf;
The aim of Farce is but to make you laugh.
Beneath the Tragick or the Comick Name,
Farces and Puppet-shows ne'er miss of Fame.
Since then, in borrow'd Dress, they've pleased the Town;
Condemn them not, appearing in their own.

Smiles we expect, from the Good-natur'd few;
As ye are done by, ye Malicious, do;
And kindly laugh at him, who laughs at you.

SONG

SONG in the First Act.

AIR, Butter'd Peafe.

Luckless *Sings.*

Does my deareft Harriot *ask*
  What for Love I wou'd purfue;
Wou'd you, Charmer, know what Task
  I wou'd undertake for you?

Ask the bold Ambitious, what
  He for Honours wou'd atchieve;
Or the gay Voluptuous, that
  Which he'd not for Pleafures give.

Ask the Mifer what he'd do
  To amafs exceffive Gain;
Or the Saint, what he'd purfue,
  His wifh'd Heav'n to attain.

Thefe I wou'd attempt, and more;
  For oh! my Harriot is to me,
All Ambition, Pleafure ftore,
  Or what Heav'n it felf can be.

Harriot *Sings.*

Wou'd my deareft Luckless *know,*
  What his Conftant Harriot *can,*
Her tender Love and Faith to fhow,
  For her dear, her only Man?

Ask the Vain Coquet, what fhe
  For Men's Adoration wou'd;
Or from Cenfure to be free,
  Ask the vile Cenforious Prude;

In a Coach and Six to ride,
  What the Mercenary Jade;
Or the Widow, to be Bride
  To a brisk, broad-fhoulder'd Blade.

All

All thefe I wou'd attempt for thee,
Cou'd I but thy Paffion fix;
Thy Tongue my fole Commander be,
And thy Arms my Coach and Six.

SONG by Mr. *Blotpage* in the Second Act.

AIR, Ye Commons and Peers.

How unhappy's the Fate
To live by one's Pate,
And be forc'd to write Hackney for Bread?
An Author's a Joke,
To all manner of Folk,
Where-ever he pops up his Head, his Head,
Where-ever he pops up his Head.

Tho' he mount on that Hack,
Old Pegafus' Back,
And of Helicon drink till he burft,
Yet a Curfe of thofe Streams,
Poetical Dreams,
They never can quench one's Thirft, &c.

Ah ! how fhou'd he fly
On Fancy fo high,
When his Limbs are in Durance and Hold?
Or how fhou'd he charm,
With Genius fo warm,
When his poor naked Body's a cold, &c.

Perfons in the FARCE.

MEN.

Lucklefs, *the Author, and Mafter of the Show,*	Mr. *Mullart,*
Witmore, *his Friend,*	Mr. *Lacy.*
Marplay, } *Comedians.*	Mr. *Reynolds,*
Sparkifh, }	Mr. *Stopler,*
Bookweight, *a Bookfeller,*	Mr. *Jones.*
Scarecrow,	Mr. *Marfhal.*
Dafh,	Mr. *Hallam.*
Quibble, } *Scriblers.*	Mr. *Dove.*
Blotpage.	Mr. *Wells,* Jun.
Jack, *Servant to* Lucklefs,	Mr. *Achurch.*
Jack-Pudding,	Mr. *Reynolds.*
Bantomite,	Mr. *Marfhal.*

WOMEN.

Mrs. Moneywood, *the Author's Landlady,*	Mrs. *Mullart,*
Harriot, *her Daughter,*	Mifs *Palms.*

Perfons

Persons in the PUPPET-SHOW.

Player,	Mr. *Dove.*
Constable,	Mr. *Wells.*
Murder-text, *a Presbyterian Parson,*	Mr. *Hallam.*
Goddess of Nonsense,	Mrs. *Mullart.*
Charon,	Mr. *Ayres.*
Curry, *a Bookseller,*	Mr. *Dove.*
A Poet,	Mr. *W. Hallam.*
Signior Opera,	Mr. *Stopler.*
Don Tragedio,	Mr. *Marshal.*
Sir Farcical Comick,	Mr. *Davenport.*
Dr. Orator,	Mr. *Jones.*
Monsieur Pantomime,	Mr. *Knott.*
Mrs. Novel,	Mrs. *Martin.*
Robgrave, *the Sexton.*	Mr. *Harris.*
Saylor,	Mr. *Achurch.*
Somebody,	Mr. *Harris,* Jun.
Nobody,	Mr. *Wells,* Jun.
Punch,	Mr. *Reynolds.*
Joan,	Mr. *Hicks.*
Lady Kingcall,	Miss *Clarke.*
Mrs. Cheat'em,	Mrs. *Wind.*
Mrs. Glass-ring,	Mrs. *Blunt.*

THE

THE
AUTHOR's FARCE.

ACT I. SCENE I.

Luckless's Room in Mrs. Moneywood's *House.*

Mrs. Moneywood, Harriot, *and* Luckless.

MONEYWOOD.

EVER tell me, Mr. *Luckless*, of your Play, and your Play.——I say, I must be paid. I would no more depend on a Benefit-Night of an un-acted Play, than I wou'd on a Benefit-Ticket in an un-drawn Lottery.——Cou'd I have guess'd that I had a Poet in my House! Cou'd I have look'd for a Poet under Lac'd Cloaths!

Luck. Why not, since you may often find Poverty under them?

Money Do you make a Jest of my Misfortune, Sir?

Luck. Rather, my Misfortune.——I am sure I have a better Title to Poverty than you.——You wallow in Wealth, and I know not where to dine.

Money Never fear that; you'll never want a Dinner

B   till

'till you have dined at all the Eating-Houſes round.——
No one ſhuts their Doors againſt you, the firſt Time
——and I think you are ſo kind, never to trouble them
a Second.

Luck. No——and if you will give me leave to walk
out of your Doors, the De'el take me if ever I come
into them again.

Money. Whenever you pleaſe, Sir; leaving your
Moveables behind.

Luck. All but my Books, dear Madam, they will be
of no Service to you.

Money. When they are ſold, Sir; and that's more
than your other Effects wou'd; for I believe you may
carry away every thing elſe in your Pockets——if you
have any.

Har. Nay, Mamma, it is barbarous to inſult him.

Money. No doubt you'll take his Part.——Pray,
get about your Buſineſs.——I ſuppoſe he intends to
pay me, by ruining you. Get you in——and if ever
I ſee you together again, I'll turn you out of Doors;
remember that.

SCENE II. Luckleſs, *and Mrs.* Moneywood.

Luck. Diſcharge all your Ill-nature on me, Madam,
but ſpare poor Miſs *Harriot.*

Money. Oh! then it is plain.——I have ſuſpected
your Familiarity a great while. You are a baſe Man.
Is it not enough to ſtay three Months in my Houſe
without paying me a Farthing, but you muſt ruin my
Child?

Luck. I love her as I love my Soul.——Had I the
World, I'd give it her all——

Money. But as you happen to have nothing in the
World, I deſire you would have nothing to ſay to her.
——I ſuppoſe you wou'd have ſettled all your Caſtles in
the Air——Oh! I wiſh you had lodg'd in one of
them, inſtead of my Houſe. Well, I am reſolv'd,

when

when you are gone away (which I heartily hope will be very foon) I'll hang over my Door in great red Letters, *No Lodgings for Poets.*——Sure, never was fuch a Gueft as you have been.——My Floor is all fpoil'd with Ink —— my Windows with Verfes, and my Door has been almoft beat down with Duns.

Luck. Wou'd your Houfe had been beaten down, and every thing, but my dear *Harriot,* crufh'd under it. Muft I be your Scolding-ftock every Morning? And becaufe my Pocket is empty, muft my Head be fill'd with Noife and Impertinence? Naturalifts fay, that all Creatures, even the moft venomous, are of fome Ufe in the Creation—— but I'm fure a Scolding Old Woman is of none; — unlefs fhe ferves in this World, as the Devil will in the other, to torment us. And if our Torment were to lie in Noife, I defy the Devil to invent a worfe.

Money. Sir, Sir ——

Luck. Madam, Madam! I will attack you at your own Weapon.——I'll pay you in your own Coin ——

Money. I wifh you wou'd pay me in any Coin, Sir.

Luck Pay you!——that Word is always uppermoft in your Mouth, as *Gelt* is in a *Dutchman's.* —— Look you, Madam, I'll do as much as a reafonable Woman can require; I'll fhew you all I have,——and give you all I have too, if you pleafe to receive it.

[*Turns his Pockets infide out.*

Money. I will not be us'd in this manner. No, Sir, I will be paid, if there be any fuch thing as Law.

Luck. By what Law you will put Money into my Pocket, I don't know; for I never heard of any one who got Money by the Law, but the Lawyers. I have told you already, Madam, and I tell you again, that the firft Money I get fhall be yours; and I have great Expectations from my Play. In the mean time, your ftaying here can be of no Service, and you may poffibly drive fome fine Thoughts out of my Head. I

muft

muſt write a Love Scene, and your Daughter wou'd be properer Company on that Occaſion, than you.

Money. You wou'd act a Love Scene, I believe, but I ſhall prevent you; for I intend to diſpoſe of my ſelf, before my Daughter.

Luck. Diſpoſe of your ſelf! to whom? to the Tallow-chandler! You will never have any thing to do with Matrimony, 'till *Hymen* turns his Torch into a Tallow-Candle; then you may be of as much Uſe to him, as a fine Lady's Eyes to *Cupid*, and may ſerve to light young People to Bed together.

Money. You are a vile Slanderer. I am not ſo old, nor ſo fat, nor ſo ugly, as you wou'd make me. And 'tis very well known, that I have had very good Offers ſince my laſt dear Husband died, if I wou'd have accepted them; —— I might have had an Attorney of *New-Inn* —— or Mr. *Fillpot* the Excise-man —— Yes, I had my Choice of two Parſons, or a Doctor of Phyſick ——— and yet I ſlighted them all; yes I ſlighted them for you. ———

Luck. For me!

Money. Yes, you have ſeen too viſible Marks of my Paſſion ——too viſible for my Reputation.

Luck. I have heard very loud Tokens of your Paſſion; but I rather took it for the Paſſion of Anger, than of Love.

Money. Oh! it aroſe from Love! —— Do but be kind, and I'll forgive thee all.

Luck Death! Madam, ſtand off. ——— If I muſt be plagu'd with you, I had rather you ſhou'd afflict my Eyes than my Touch; at a diſtance, you offend but one Senſe; but nearer, you offend them all —— and I wou'd ſooner loſe them all, than undergo you.

Money. You ſhall repent this, Sir, remember that—— you ſhall repent it.——I'll ſhew you the Revenge of an injur'd Woman.

Luck. I ſhall never repent any thing that rids me of you, Madam, I aſſure you. [*Exit.*

SCENE

SCENE III. Luckless, Harriot.

Har. My dear *Harry*, I have been waiting an Opportunity to return to you.

Luck. My dear *Harriot*——come to my Arms, and let me lay my aking, sick Head on thy tender Bosom.

Har. What's the Matter, my Dear?

Luck. I am sick of the most abominable Distemper.

Har. Heaven forbid! What is it?

Luck. Poverty, my Love——and your Mother is a most excellent Nurse.

Har. What shall I do for you? My Money is all gone, and so are my Cloaths; which, when my Mother finds out, I shall have as much need of a Surgeon, as you can have now of a Doctor.

Luck. No, I wou'd sooner starve, or beg, or steal, or die, than one Hair of my dear *Harriot* shou'd be hurt. I am armed against her utmost Rage; but for you I fear; for such a Spirit as your Mother, no *Amazon* ever possess'd before. So, if my present Design succeeds, we will leave her together——

Har. But if it shou'd fail——

Luck, Say, then, my *Harriot*, wou'd my Charmer fly
To the cold Climes beneath the Polar Sky?
Or, arm'd with Love; cou'd she endure to sweat,
Beneath the sultry, dry *Æquator's* Heat?
Thirst, Hunger, Labour, Hardship, could she prove,
From Conversation of the World remove,
And only know the Joys of constant Love?

Har. Oh! more than this, my *Luckless*, would I do:
All Places are a Heaven, when with you:
Let me repose but on that faithful Breast,
Give me thy Love————the World may take the rest.

Luck.

Luck. My dear *Harriot!* by Heav'n, thy Lips are ſweeter than the Honey, and thy Temper is yet ſweeter than them.

Har. [*Sighs.*]

Luck. Why do you ſigh, my Sweet?

Har. I only wiſh I were aſſured of the Sincerity of your Love.   [*A Song.*

Luck. It is unkind in you to doubt it. —— I wiſh it was in my Power to give you greater Proofs —— but I will give you the greateſt in my Power —— which is, to marry you this Inſtant.

Har. Then I am eaſy : But it is better to delay that 'till our Circumſtances alter ——— for, remember what you have your ſelf ſaid in the Song you taught me :

> *Wou'd you the charming Queen of Love,*
>   *Invite with you to dwell ;*
> *No Want your Poverty ſhou'd prove,*
>   *No State your Riches tell.*

> *Both Her, and Happineſs to hold,*
>   *A middle State muſt pleaſe ;*
> *They ſhun the Houſe that ſhines with Gold,*
>   *And that which ſhines with Greaſe.*

Money. [*Within.*] Harriot! Harriot!

Har. Hear the dreadful Summons ; Adieu, my Dear. I will take the firſt Opportunity of ſeeing you again.

Luck. Adieu to my pretty Charmer! ——— Go thy ways, for the firſt of thy Sex. What Fool wou'd dangle after, and make himſelf a Slave to the inſolent Pride of a Miſtreſs, when he may find another with as much Good-nature as he wou'd wiſh?

SCENE

SCENE IV. Luckless, Jack.

So! What News bring you!

Jack. An't pleafe your Honour, I have been at my Lord's, and his Lordfhip thanks you for the Favour you have offered of reading your Play to him; but he has fuch a prodigious deal of Bufinefs, he begs to be excus'd.——I have been with Mr. *Keyber* too; he made me no Anfwer at all. — Mr. *Bookweight* will be here immediately,

Luck. Jack!

Jack. Sir.

Luck. Fetch my Hat hither.

Jack. It is here, Sir.

Luck. Carry it to the Pawn-broker's. And, in your way home, call at the Cook's-Shop——make Hafte. So, one way or other I find, my Head muft always provide for my Belly.

SCENE V. Luckless, Witmore. ·

Luck. I am furprized, —— dear *Witmore!*

Wit. Dear *Harry!*

Luck. This is kind, indeed; but I do not more wonder at finding a Man in this Age, who can be a Friend to Adverfity, than that Fortune fhould be fo much my Friend, as to direct you to me; for fhe is a Lady I have not been much indebted to lately.

Wit. She who told me, I affure you, is one you have been indebted to a long while.

Luck. Whom do you mean?

Wit. One who complains of your Unkindnefs in not Vifiting her—— Mrs. *Lovewood.*

Luck. Doft thou vifit there ftill, then?

Wit. I throw an idle Hour away there fometimes— when I am in an ill Humour, I go there and rail,

where

where I am fure to feed it with all the Scandal in Town——— No News-writer *is* more diligent in procuring Intelligence——— no Bawd in looking after Girls with an uncrack'd Maiden-head, than fhe in fearching out Women with crack'd Reputations.

Luck. The much more infamous Office of the two.

Wit. Thou art ftill a Favourer of the Women, I find.

Luck. Ay, the Women and the Mufes——— the high Roads to Beggary.

Wit. What, art thou not cured of Scribling yet?

Luck. No, Scribling is as impoffible to cure as the Gout.

Wit. And as fure a Sign of Poverty as the Gout of Riches. S'death! in an Age of Learning and true Politenefs, where a Man might fucceed by his Merit, it wou'd be an Encouragement.——— But now, when Party and Prejudice carry all before them, when Learning is decried, Wit not underftood, when the Theatres are Puppet-Shows, and the Comedians Ballad-Singers: When Fools lead the Town, wou'd a Man think to thrive by his Wit?——— If you muft write, write Nonfenfe, write Opera's, write Entertainments, write *Hurlo-thrumbo's*——— Set up an *Oratory* and preach Nonfenfe; and you may meet with Encouragement enough. If you wou'd receive Applaufe, deferve to receive Sentence at the *Old-Baily·* And if you wou'd ride in your Coach, deferve to ride in a Cart.

Luck You are warm, my Friend.

Wit. It is becaufe I am your Friend. I cannot bear to hear the Man I love ridiculed by Fools and Idiots——— To fee a Fellow, who had he been born a *Chinefe,* had been fome low Mechanick, tofs up his empty Noddle with a fcornful Difdain of what he has not underftood; and Women abufing what they have neither feen nor read, from an unreafonable Prejudice to an honeft Fellow, whom they have not known. If thou wilt write againft all thefe Reafons get a Patron,

be

be Pimp to fome worthlefs Man of Quality, write Panegyricks on him, flatter him with as many Virtues as he has Vices—— and don't pretend to ftand thy felf againft a Tide of Prejudice and Ill-nature, which would have over-whelm'd a *Plato* or a *Socrates.*

Luck. I own thy Advice is friendly, and I fear too much Truth is on your Side—— but what wou'd you advife me to do?

Wit. Thou art a vigorous young Fellow—— and there are rich Widows in Town.

Luck. But I am already engaged.

Wit. Why don't you marry then—— for I fuppofe you are not fo mad, to have any Engagement with a poor Miftrefs.

Luck. Even fo, faith, and fo heartily that I wou'd not change her for the Widow of a *Crœfus.*

Wit. Now thou art undone, indeed. Matrimony clenches Ruin beyond Retrieval. What unfortunate Stars wert thou born under! Was it not enough to follow thofe nine ragged Jades the Mufes, but you muft faften on fome Earth-born Miftrefs as poor as them?

Luck. Fie *Witmore,* thou art grown a Churl.

Wit. While thou wert happy, I cou'd bear thefe Flights; while thy Rooms were furnifhed, and thy Cloaths whole, I cou'd bear thee.——But for a Man to preach up Love and the Mufes in a Garret, it wou'd not make me more fick to hear Honefty talked of at Court, Confcience at *Weftminfter,* Politenefs at the Univerfity—— Nay, I had rather hear Women difputing on the Mathematicks————

———

SCENE VI. Lucklefs, Witmore, Bookweight.

Luck Mr *Bookweight,* your very humble Servant.

Book. I was told, Sir, you had particular Bufinefs with me,

Luck.

Luck. Yes, Mr. *Bookweight*, I have fomething to put into your Hands. I have a Play for you, Mr. *Bookweight*.

Book. Is it accepted, Sir?

Luck. Not yet.

Book. Oh! Sir! when it is, it will be then Time enough to talk about it. A Play, like a Bill, is of no Value before it is accepted, nor indeed when it is, very often. This too is a plentiful Year of Plays —— and they are like Nuts: In a plentiful Year they are commonly very bad.

Luck. But fuppofe it were accepted (as you term it) what wou'd you give me for it? (not that I want Money, Sir——)

Book. No, Sir, certainly—— But before I can make any Anfwer I muft read it—— I cannot offer any thing for what I do not know the Value of.

Wit. That I imagine granted by the Players Approbation: For they are, you know, very great Judges.

Book. Yes, Sir, that they are, indeed—— That they muft be allowed to be, as being Men of great Learning: But a Play which will do for them, will not always do for us.——There are your Acting Plays, and your Reading Plays.

Wit. I do not underftand that Diftinction.

Book. Why, Sir, your Acting Play is entirely fupported by the Merit of the Actor, without any Regard to the Author at all ·—— In this Cafe, it fignifies very little whether there be any Senfe in it or no. Now your Reading Play is of a different Stamp, and muft have Wit and Meaning in it—— Thefe latter I call your Subftantive, as being able to fupport themfelves. The former are your Adjective, as what require the Buffoonry and Geftures of an Actor to be joined to them, to fhew their Signification

Luck. Very learnedly defin'd, truly, Mr *Bookweight*.

Book. I hope I have not had fo much Learning go through my Hands without leaving fome in my Head.

Luck.

Luck. Well: But, Mr. *Bookweight,* I hope you will advance fomething——

Book Why, had you a great Reputation I might venture: But, truly, for young Beginners it is a very great Hazard: For, indeed, the Reputation of the Author carries the greateft Sway in thefe Affairs. The Town have been fo fond of fome Authors, that they have run them up to Infallibility, and wou'd have applauded them even againft their Senfes.

Wit. And who but a Mad-man would write in fuch an Age?

Luck. S'death! *Witmore!* 'Tis cruel to infult my Misfortunes.

Wit. I wou'd cure them—— and that is not to be done by Lenitives.

Book. I am of that Gentleman's Opinion: I do think writing the filleft Thing a Man can undertake.

Luck. 'Tis ftrange you fhou'd fay fo, who live by it.

Book. Live by it! Ah! If you had loft as much by Writers as I have done, you wou'd be of my Opinion.

Luck, But we are lofing Time—— Will you advance fifty Guineas on my Play?

Book. No—nor fifty Shillings, I affure you.

Luck. S'death! Sir; do you beat me down at this Rate?

Book. Sir, I wou'd not give you fifty Farthings—— Fifty Guineas, indeed! your Name is well worth that.

Luck Jack ——   [Jack *enters.*
Take this worthy Gentleman and kick him down Stairs.

Book. Sir, I fhall make you repent this——

Jack. Come, Sir, will you pleafe to brufh——

Book. Help— Murder— I'll have the Law of you, Sir.

Luck. Ha, ha, ha.——

SCENE

SCENE VII. Luckless, Witmore, *Mrs.* Moneywood.

Money. What Noise is this? It is a very fine Thing truly, Mr. *Luckless,* that you will make these Uproars in my House.———

Luck. If you dislike it, it is in your Power to drown a much greater. Do you but speak, Madam, and I am sure no one will be heard but your self

Money. Very well, indeed! fine Reflections on my Character!—— Sir, Sir, all the Neighbours know that I have been as quiet a Woman as any in the Parish. I had no Noises in my House till you came. We were the Family of Love——But you have been a Nusance to the whole Neighbourhood———— While you had Money my Doors were thundered at every Morning at four and five, and since you have had none, my Walls have echoed nothing but your Noise and your Poetry———— Then there's the Rascal your Man—— but I'll pay the Dog——— I'll scour him——— [*to* Wit.] Sir, I am glad you are a Witness to his Abuses of me———

Wit. I am a Witness indeed, Madam, how unjustly he has abus'd you.

Luck. [Jack *whispers.*] *Witmore,* you'll excuse me a Moment.

SCENE VIII. *Mrs.* Moneywood, Witmore.

Money. Yes, Sir; and Sir, a Man that has never shewn one the Colour of his Money.

Wit. Very hard, truly——— How much may he be in your Debt, pray? Because he has order'd me to pay you.

Money. Ah! Sir, I wish he had.

Wit.

Wit. I am ferious, I affure you.

Money. I am very glad to hear it, Sir. Here is the Bill as we fettled it this very Morning. I always thought indeed Mr. *Lucklefs* had a good deal of Honefty in his Principles—any Man may be unfortunate: but I knew when he had Money I fhou'd have it—I never was in any Fear for my Money, for my Part.

Wit. There, Madam, is your Money on the Table. Pleafe to write a Receipt only.

Money. Sir, I give you a great many Thanks. There, Sir, is the Receipt——Well, if Mr. *Lucklefs* was but a little Soberer——I fhou'd like him for a Lodger exceedingly: for I muft fay I think him a very pleafant good-natur'd Man.

SCENE IX. Lucklefs *returns.*

Luck. Thofe are Words I never heard out of that Mouth before.

Money. Ha, ha, ha! you are pleas'd to be Merry.

Luck. Why *Witmore,* thou haft the Faculty oppofite to that of a Witch——and can'ft lay a Tempeft. I fhou'd have as foon imagin'd one Man cou'd have ftopt a Cannon Ball in its full Force, as her Tongue, and I believe fhe may be heard as far——Were fhe to roar forth a Summons to a Town, it wou'd have more Effect on the Governor than a volley of Artillery.

Money. Ha, ha, ha!

Wit. *Lucklefs,* good Morrow——I will fee you again foon——

Luck. *Witmore,* I am yours.

SCENE X. Lucklefs, *Mrs.* Moneywood.

Money. Well, Mr *Lucklefs,* you are a comical Man, to give one fuch a Character to a Stranger.

Luck.

Luck. The Company is gone, Madam; and now, like true Man and Wife, we may fall to abufing one another as faft as we pleafe.

Money. Abufe me as you will, fo you pay me, Sir.

Luck. S' Death! Madam, I will pay you

Money. Nay, Sir, I do not afk it before it is due—— I don't queftion your Payment at all: If you were to ftay in my Houfe this Quarter of a Year, as I hope you will, I fhou'd not afk you for a Farthing.

Luck. Tol, lol, lol.——But I fhall have her begin with her Paffion immediately; and I had rather feel the higheft Effects of her Rage, than the lighteft of her Love.

Money. But why did you chufe to furprize me with my Money? why did you not tell me you'd pay me?

Luck. Why have I not told you!

Money. Yes, you told me of a Play and Stuff: But you never told me you wou'd order a Gentleman to pay me. Well, you have comical ways with you: but you have Honefty in the Bottom, and I'm fure the Gentleman himfelf will own I gave you that Character.

Luck. Oh!——I fmell you now——You fee, Madam, I am better than my Word to you; did he pay it you in Gold or Silver?

Money. All pure Gold.

Luck. I have a vaft deal of Silver within; will you do me the favour of taking it in Silver? that may be of ufe to you in the Shop too.

Money. Any thing to oblige you, Sir!

Luck. *Jack,* bring out the great Bag number *One.* Pleafe to tell the Money, Madam, on that Table.

Money. [*Tells the Money.*] It's eafily told——Heaven knows there's not fo much on't.

Enter Jack.

[*When* Jack *enters,* Lucklefs *gets between Mrs.* Money-wood *and the Table.*]

Jack. Sir, the Bag is fo heavy, I cannot bring it in.

Luck.

Luck. Why then, come and help to thrust a heavier Bag out.

Money. What do you mean, Sir?

Luck. Only to pay you in my Bedchamber.

Money. Villain, Dog, I'll swear a Robbery and have you hang'd: Rogues, Villains!

Luck. [*Shuts the Door.*] Be as noisy as you please.—
Jack, call a Coach, and d'ye hear, get up behind it and attend me.

The End of the First Act.

A C T

ACT II. SCENE I.

A *Tavern.*

Luckless, Marplay, Sparkish.

LUCKLESS [*Reads.*]

THEN hence my Sorrows, hence my ev'ry Fear;
   No matter where, fo we are blefs'd together.
With thee, the barren Rocks, where not one ftep
Of human Race lies printed in the Snow,
   Look lovely as the fmiling Infant Spring.

Mar. [*Yawning.*] Will you pleafe to read that again, Sir?

Luck. [*Reads again.*]

Mar. Then hence my Sorrow——Horror is a much better Word, in my Opinion—— And then in the fecond Line——will you pleafe to read it again.

Luck. No matter where, fo we are blefs'd together.

Mar. In my Opinion it wou'd be better fo:
No matter where, fo fomewhere we're together.
Where is the Queftion, fomewhere is the Anfwer——
Read on, Sir.

Luck. [*Reads on.*] With thee, &c.

Mar. I cou'd alter thofe Lines to a much better Idea.
   With thee, the barren Blocks, [*That is Trees.*]
      where not a bit
Of human Face is painted on the Bark,
   Look green as *Covent-Garden* in the Spring.

Luck. Green as *Covent-Garden!*

Mar. Yes, *Covent-Garden* Market: where they fell Greens.

                                             Luck.

Luck. Monſtrous! Sir, I muſt ask your Pardon, I cannot conſent to ſuch an Alteration. It is downright Nonſenſe.

Mar. [*Riſing from the Table.*] Sir, it will not do——and ſo I wou'd not have you think any more of it.

Spark. No, no, no. It will not do.

Luck. What Faults do you find?

Mar. Sir, there is nothing in it that pleaſes me, ſo I am ſure there is nothing in it that will pleaſe the Town.

Spark. There is nothing in it that will pleaſe the Town.

Luck. Methinks you ſhou'd find ſome particular Fault.

Mar. Truly, Sir, it is ſo full of Faults——that the Eye of my Judgment is ſo diſtracted with the Variety of Objects that it cannot fix on any.

Spark. No, no, no —— cannot fix on any.

Mar. In ſhort, there is not one good thing in it from the Beginning to the End.

Luck. Some who have read it think otherwiſe.

Mar. Let them think as they pleaſe——I'm ſure we are the beſt Judges.

Spark. Yes, yes, we are the beſt Judges.

Luck. Cou'd you convince me of any Fault, I wou'd amend it: but you argue in Plays as the Pope does in Religion, or the *Ariſtotleiſts* in Philoſophy; you maintain your Hypotheſis by an *Ipſe dicit.*

Mar. I don't underſtand your hard Words, Sir; but I think it is very hard if a Man who has been ſo long in a Trade as I have, ſhou'd not underſtand the Value of his Merchandize: ſhou'd not know what Goods will beſt pleaſe the Town. —— Come —— *Sparkiſh,* will you go to *Toms!*

Luck. Fare ye well, Gentlemen: may another Play do you more Service.

C

SCENE

SCENE II.   Marplay, Sparkish.

Mar. Ha, ha, ha!

Spark. What doſt think of the Play?

Mar. It may. be a very good one, for ought I know; but I know the Author has no Intereſt.

Spark. Give me Intereſt, and rat the Play. ——

Mar. Rather rat the Play which has no Intereſt. Intereſt ſways as much in the Theatre as at Court. —— And you know it is not always the Companion of Merit in either.

Spark. But pray, Mr. *Marplay*, what was the Reaſon of that extraordinary Demand of yours upon the Office?

Mar. Truly, Sir, it was for the Good of the Office. —— Some of it was given to Puffs, to cry up our new Plays —— And one half Guinea to Mr. *Scribler* for a Panegyrical Eſſay in the News-Paper, with ſome other ſuch Services. But have you ſeen my new Entertainment practiſed, *Cuckolds all a Row?*

Spark. No.

Mar. I will affirm this, that it is the beſt thing that has ever appear'd on the Stage —— I don't know whether I ſhall not lay the Pit and Boxes together, at half a Guinea a Seat.

Spark. I wou'd not adviſe that: for the Town grumbles at our raiſing the Prices as we have done.

Mar. Rat the Town. —— Let them grumble, I'm ſure they will not ſtay away —— For their Hiſſes —— they have no more Effect on me than Muſick wou'd have on an Owl —— or the Curſes of an undone Client on an Attorney —— I have been us'd to them; and any Man who loves hiſſing may have his three Shillings worth at me whenever he pleaſes.

SCENE

SCENE III. *A Room in Mr.* Bookweight's *House.*

Dash, Blotpage, Quibble, *writing at several Tables.*

Dash. Pox on't, I'm as dull as an Ox, tho' I have not a bit of one within me.—I have not din'd these two Days, and yet my Head is as heavy as any Alderman's or Lord's. I carry about me Symbols of all the Elements; my Head is as heavy as Water, my Pockets are light as Air, my Appetite is as hot as Fire, and my Coat is as dirty as Earth.

Blot Lend me your *Byshe*, Mr. *Dash*, I want a Rhime for Wind.———

Dash. Why there! blind, and kind, and behind, and find, and Mind—It is one of the easiest Terminations imaginable; I have had it four times in a Page.

Blot. Devil take the first Inventor of Rhiming I say. Your Business is much easier, Mr. *Dash.* Well, of all the Places in my Master's Gift—I shou'd most like to be Clerk of the Ghosts and Murders. You have nothing to do but to put a set of terrible Words together in the Title Page.

Dash. The Business is easy enough, but it is at a very low Ebb now. No, Mr *Quibble* there, as Clerk of the Libels, wou'd have the best Place, were it not that few Men ever sat in his Chair long without standing on an odd sort of a Stool in the Street, to be gap'd at an Hour or two by the Mob.

Quib. We act on different Principles, Mr. *Dash*; 'tis your Business to promise more than you perform, and mine to promise less.

Blot. Pshaw! thy Business is to perform nothing at all.

Dash. It becomes an Author to be Diffusive in his Title Page. A Title Page is to a Book, what a fine Neck is to a Woman—Therefore ought to be the most regarded, as it is the Part which is view'd before the Purchase. [*A Song.*

SCENE IV. *To them*, Bookweight.

Book. Fie upon it Gentlemen! what, not at your Pens? Do you confider, Mr. *Quibble*, that it is above a Fortnight fince your Letter from a Friend in the Country was publifh'd. ——Is it not high time for an Anfwer to come out —— at this rate, before your Anfwer is Printed your Letter will be forgot —— I love to keep a Controverfy up warm —— I have had Authors who have writ a Pamphlet in the Morning, anfwered it in the Afternoon, and compromifed the matter at Night.

Quib. Sir, I will be as expeditious as poffible.

Book. Well, Mr. *Dafh*, have you done that Murder yet?

Dafk. Yes, Sir, the Murder is done —— I am only about a few moral Reflections to place before it.

Book. Very well ——then let me have the Ghoft finifh'd by this Day Sevennight.

Dafh. What fort of a Ghoft wou'd you have, Sir? the laft was a pale one.

Book. Then let this be a bloody one.—— Mr. *Blotpage*, what have your Lucubrations produc'd? —— [*reads*] Poetical Advice to a certain —— from a certain ——on a certain —— from a certain —— Very good! I will fay, Mr. *Blotpage* writes as good a Dafh as any Man in *Europe*.

SCENE V. *To them*, Index.

So, Mr. *Index*, what News with you?

Ind. I have brought my Bill, Sir.

Book. What's here?——for adapting the Motto of *Rifum teneatis Amici* to a dozen Pamphlets —— at Six Pence *per* each — Six Shillings.

For *Omnia vincit amor & nos cedamus Amori* —— Six Pence. For *Difficile eft Satyram non fcribere* —— Six Pence

Pence. Hum, hum, hum —— ah —— a Sum Total, for Thirty Six *Latin* Mottos, *Eighteen Shillings* ; *ditto English* Seven, *One Shilling* and *Nine Pence* ; *ditto Greek* Four, *One Shilling*. Why, Friend, are your *Latin* Mottos dearer than your *Greek* ?

Ind. Yes marry are they, Sir : for as no body now understands *Greek*, so I may use any Sentence in that Language, to whatsoever purpose I please.

Book. You shall have your Money immediately : and pray remember that I must have two *Latin* Sedition Mottos, and one *Greek* Moral Motto, for Pamphlets, by To-morrow Morning.

Quib. I want two *Latin* Sentences Sir, one for Page the Fourth, in the Praise of Virtue ; and the other for Page the Tenth, in the Praise of Beauty.

Book Let me have those too.

Ind. Sir, I shall take care to provide them.

―――――――――――――――――――――――

SCENE VI. Bookweight, Dash, Blotpage, Quibble, Scarecrow.

Scare. Sir, I have brought you a Libel against the Ministry.

Book. Sir, I shall not take any thing against them (for I have two in the Press already.)   [*Aside.*

Scare. Then, Sir, I have another in Defence of them.

Book. Sir, I never take any thing in Defence of Power.

Scare. I have a Translation of *Virgil's Æneid*, with Notes on it.

Book. That, Sir, is what I do not care to venture on —— you may try by Subscription, if you please : but I wou'd not advise you : for that Bubble is almost down : People begin to be afraid of Authors, since they have writ and acted like Stock-Jobbers. So to oblige a young Beginner, I don't care if I Print it at my own Expence.

Scare.

Scare. But pray, Sir, at whose Expence shall I eat?

Book. That's an empty Question.

Scare It comes from an empty Stomach, I'm sure.

Book From an empty Head, I'm afraid. Are there not a thousand ways for a Man to get his Bread by ?

Scare. I wish you wou'd put me into one.

Book. Why then, Sir, I wou'd advise you to come and take your Seat at my Tables. Here will be every thing that is necessary provided for you. I am as great a Friend to Learning as the *Dutch* are to Trade. —— No one can want Bread with me, who will earn it. Besides, a Translator will be of use to me : for my last is in *Newgate* for Shoplifting. The Rogue had gotten a trick of translating out of the Shops as well as out of the Languages.

Scare. I prefer any thing to starving.

Book Then, Sir, if you please to throw by your Hat, which you will have no more use for, and take up your Pen.

Scare. But, Sir, I am afraid I am not qualified for a Translator.

Book. How, not qualified !

Scare. No, Sir : I understand no Language but my own.

Book What, and translate *Virgil ?*

Scare. Alas, Sir, I translated him out of *Dryden.*

Book. Not qualified ! ——If I was an Emperor thou should'st be my Prime Minister. Thou art as well veis'd in thy Trade, as if thou had'st labour'd in my Garret these ten Years. —— Let me tell you, Friend, you will have more occasion for Invention than Learning here · you will be sometimes obliged to translate Books out of all Languages (especially *French*) which were never Printed in any Language whatsoever.

Scare. Your Trade abounds in Mysteries.

Book. The Study of Bookselling is as difficult as the Law, —— and there are as many Tricks in the one as the other. Sometimes we give a Foreign Name to our own

Labour

Labour — and fometimes we put our own Names to the Labour of others. Then as the Lawyers have *John-a-Nokes* and *Tom-a-Stiles*, fo we have Meffieurs *Moore* near St. *Paul's*, and *Smith* near the *Royal Exchange*.

SCENE VII. *To them,* Luckless.

Luck. Mr. *Bookweight*, your Servant. Who can form to himfelf an Idea more amiable than of a Man at the Head of fo many Patriots working for the Benefit of their Country?

Book. Truly, Sir, I believe it is an Idea more agreeable to you ——— than that of a Gentleman in the *Crown-Office* paying thirty or forty Guineas for abufing an honeft Tradefman.

Luck. Pfhaw, that was only jocofely done, and a Man who lives by Wit, muft not be angry at a Jeft ; befides, the Law has been your Enemy ——— and you wou'd not fly to an Enemy for Succour.

Book. Sir, I will ufe my Enemy as I wou'd my Friend, for my own Ends : But pray, Sir, what has brought you hither? If you have a mind to compromife the Matter, I had rather have a little of your Money, than that the Lawyers fhou'd have a great deal.

Luck. Haft thou dealt in Paper fo long, and talk of Money to a modern Author? You might as well have talk'd *Latin* or *Greek* to him. I have brought you Paper, Sir.

Book. That is not bringing me Money, I own ——— but it fhall not be taking away Money, Sir, for I will have nothing to do with your Paper or you either.

Luck. Why pr'ythee, Man, I have not brought you a Play ——— nor a Sermon.

Book. Have you brought me an Opera?

Luck. You may call it an Opera if you will, but I call it a Puppet-Show.

Book. A Puppet-Show !

Luck.

Luck. Ay, a Puppet-Show, and is to be play'd this Night in the *Haymarket* Play-House.

Book. A Puppet-Show in a Play-House!

Luck. What have been all the Play-Houses a long time but Puppet-Shows?

Book Why, I don't know but it may succeed; at least, I had rather venture on a thing of that nature, than a regular Play —— so if you please to come in, if I can make a Bargain with you I will —— Gentlemen, you may go to Dinner.

SCENE VIII. *The Street.*

Enter Jack-Pudding, *Drummer and Mob. The Drum ceasing.*

Har. This is to give Notice to all Gentlemen, Ladies and others —— that at the Play-House opposite to the Opera in the *Haymarket,* this Evening will be perform'd the whole Puppet-Show call'd *The Pleasures of the Town;* in which will be shewn the whole Court of Dulness, with abundance of Singing and Dancing, and several other Entertainments —— also the Comical and diverting Humours of Some-body, and No-body : *Punch* and his Wife *Joan,* to be perform'd by living Figures —— some of them Six foot high —— beginning exactly at Seven a Clock. God save the King. [*Drum beats.*

SCENE IX. Witmore *with a* Paper, Luckless *meeting.*

Wit. Oh! *Luckless,* I am overjoy'd at meeting you —— here, take this Paper, and you will be discourag'd from Writing, I warrant you.

Luck. What is it? —— Oh! one of my Play-Bills.

Wit. One of thy Play-Bills!

Luck Even so, Sir! —— I have taken the Advice you gave me this Morning. *Wit.*

Wit. Explain.

Luck. Why, I had fome time fince given this Puppet-Show of mine to be Rehearfed, and the Actors were all perfect in their Parts; but we happen'd to diffent about fome Particulars, and I had a defign to have given it over; 'till having my Play refus'd by *Marplay* and *Sparkifh*, I fent for the Managers of the Houfe in a Paffion, join'd Iffue with them, and this very Evening it is to be acted.

Wit. Well—I wifh you Succefs.——

Luck. Where are you going?

Wit. Any where but to hear you damn'd, which I muft, if I were to go to your Puppet-Show——I tell you the Town is prejudic'd againft you, and they will damn you, whether you deferve it or no.——If they fhou'd laugh till they burft——the moment they knew you were the Author——they wou'd change their Faces, and fwear they never laugh'd at all.

Luck. Pfhaw, I can't believe thee.

Wit. 'Sdeath! I have heard Senfe run down, and feen Idiotifm, downright Idiotifm triumph fo often, that I cou'd almoft think of Wit and Folly as Mr. *Hobbes* does of Moral Good and Evil, that there are no fuch Things.

Luck. Well, indulge me in this Trial——and I affure thee if it be fuccefslefs it fhall be the laft.

Wit. On that Condition I will——but fhou'd the Torrent run againft you, I fhall be a fafhionable Friend, and hifs with the reft.

Luck. No, a Man who cou'd do fo unfafhionable and fo generous a thing, as Mr. *Witmore* did this Morning.——

Wit. In return, will you grant me a Favour?

Luck. Do you doubt it?

Wit Never mention it to me more——I will now to the Pit.——

Luck. And I behind the Scenes.

SCENE

SCENE X. *Mrs.* Honeywood's.

Mrs. Honeywood, *and* Harriot.

Har. It is very hard, Madam, that you will not suffer me at least to indulge my self in Grief; that it is not enough to tear me from the Man I love, but I must have my Ears eternally curst with hearing him abused——

Mrs. Mon. Oh monstrous! Love a Puppet-Show Fellow!

Har. His Misfortunes may lessen him in the Eye of the World: But they shall never lessen him in mine, Nay, I love him for them.

Mrs. Mon. You have not a drop of my Blood in you. Love a Man for his Misfortune!——Huffy, to be poor and unfortunate are Crimes —— Riches are the only Recommendations to People of Sense of both Sexes, and a Coach and Six is one of the *Cardinal Virtues.*

Har. I despise it, and the Fool who was born to it. No, give me the Man, who, thrown naked upon the World, like my dear *Luckless,* can make his way through it by his Merit and virtuous Industry.

Mrs. Mon. Virtuous Industry! A very virtuous, industrious Gentleman, truly. He hath robbed me of a few Guineas To-day or so —— but he is a very virtuous Man no doubt.

Har. He hath only borrowed what you know he will repay:——you know he is honest.

Mrs. Mon. I am no more satisfied of his Honesty than you can be of his Love.

Har. Which I am sure he hath given me sufficient Proofs of.

Mrs. Mon. Proofs! Oh the Villain! Hath he given you Proofs of Love?

Har. All that a modest Woman can require.

Mrs. Mon. If he hath given you all a modest Wo
man

man can require, I am afraid he has given you more than a modeſt Woman ſhould take: Becauſe he hath been ſo good a Lodger, I ſuppoſe I ſhall have ſome more of the Family to keep: It is probable I may live to ſee half a dozen Grandſons of mine in *Grubſtreet*.

Enter Jack.

So, Raſcal, what's become of your Maſter?

Jack Oh, Madam! I am frightned out of my Wits.

Mon. }
Har. } What's the matter?

Jack. There's the ſtrangeſt ſort of Man below enquiring after my Maſter, that ever was ſeen.

Mon. What, I ſuppoſe a ſort of Bailiff?

Jack. Oh! Madam, I fancy it is the Man in the Moon, or ſome Monſter —— there are five hundred People at the Door looking at him —— he is dreſſed up in nothing but Ruffles and Cabbage Nets.

Mon. This is either ſome Trick of his to catch me, or ſome Trick of a Bailiff to catch him —— However, I'll go fift out the bottom of it. Come, ſhew me where he is.

Har. Heav'ns protect my dear *Luckleſs*.

The End of the Second Act.

A C T

ACT III. SCENE I.

The Play-House.

Enter Luckless *as* Master *of the Show, and* Player.

Mast. IT'S very surprizing, that after I have been at all this Expence and Trouble to set up my Things in your House, you should desire me to Recant; and now too, when the Spectators are all assembled, and will either have the Show or their Money.

Play. It is beneath the Dignity of the Stage.

Mast. That may be, so is all Farce, and yet you see a Farce brings more Company to a House than the best Play that ever was writ——For this Age would allow *Tom Durfey* a better Poet than *Congreve* or *Wycherly*; who would not then rather Eat by his Nonsense, than Starve by his Wit — The Lodgings of Wits have long been in the Air, and Air must be their Food now-a-days.

Play. I am not the first indeed that has disgrac'd the Stage.

Mast. And I heartily wish you may be the last, and that my Puppet-Show may expell Farce and Opera, as they have done Tragedy and Comedy.

Play But hark you Friend, how came you to call this Performance of yours a Puppet-Show?

Mast You must know, Sir, that it was originally design'd to be play'd by real Puppets, till a Friend of mine observing the Success of some things in Town, advis'd me to bring it on the Stage. I had offer'd it to the old House, but they say nothing but your fine

Sense

Senſe, ſuch Plays as *Cæſar* in *Ægypt*, will go down there.

Play. But what is the Deſign or Plot? for I could make neither Head nor Tail of it, for my part.

Maſt. Why Sir, the Goddeſs of *Nonſenſe* is to fall in Love with the Ghoſt of Signior *Opera*.

Play. Fall in Love with a Ghoſt, ha, ha, ha!

Maſt. Ay Sir——You muſt know that the Scene is laid on the other ſide of the River *Styx*, ſo all the People of the Play are Ghoſts.

Play. This Marrying of Ghoſts is a new Doctrine, Friend.

Maſt. So much the likelier to pleaſe——Tho' I can't ſay but I took the hint of this Thing from the old Houſe, who obſerving that every one could not ſee the real Coronation brought a Repreſentation of it upon their Stage——So Sir, ſince every one has not Time or Opportunity to viſit all the Diverſions of the Town, I have brought moſt of them together in one ——But come, it is time to begin. I think we will have an Overture, tho' ours be not a regular Opera.

Play. By all means an Overture.

Maſt If you pleaſe, Sir, you ſhall ſit down by me. Play away.

Maſt Gentlemen, the firſt thing I preſent you with is *Punchinello*.

[*The Curtain drawn diſcovers* Punch *in a great Chair.*

Punch *Sings.*

A I R I. Whilſt the Town's brimfull of Folly.

Whilſt the Town's brimfull of Farces,
Flocking whilſt we ſee her Aſſes
Thick as Grapes upon a Bunch,
Criticks, whilſt you ſmile on Madneſs,
And more ſtupid, ſolemn Sadneſs;
Sure you will not frown on Punch.

Maſt.

Maſt. The next is *Punch's* Wife *Joan.*

Enter Joan.

Joan. What can ail my Husband? he is continually humming Tunes, tho' his Voice be only fit to warble at *Hogg's Norton*, where the Piggs would accompany it with Organs. I was in hopes Death would have ſtopp'd his Mouth at laſt——But he keeps his old harmonious Humour even in the Shades.

Punch. Be not angry, dear *Joan;* *Orpheus* obtain'd his Wife from the Shades, by charming *Pluto* with his Muſick.

Joan Sirrah, Sirrah, ſhould *Pluto* hear you Sing you could expect no leſs Puniſhment than *Tantalus* has, ——Nay the Waters would be brought above your Mouth, to ſtop it.

Punch. Truly, Madam, I don't wiſh the ſame Succeſs *Orpheus* met with; could I gain my own Liberty—— the Devil might have you with all my Heart.

A I R II.

Joan, Joan, Joan, *has a Thundring Tongue,*
And Joan, Joan, Joan, *is a bold one.*
   How happy is he,
   Who from Wedlock is free:
For who'd have a Wife to Scold one?

Joan. Punch, Punch, Punch, *pr'ythee think of your*
       Hunch,
Pr'ythee look at your great ſtrutting Belly:
   Sirrah, if you dare
   War with me declare,
I will beat your fat Gutts to a Jelly.

[Here they Dance.

A I R

AIR III. Bobbing *Joan.*

Pun. Joan, *you are the Plague of my Life,*
  A Rope would be welcomer than such a Wife.
Joan. Punch, *your Merits had you but shar'd,*
  Your Neck had been longer by half a Yard:
Pun. *Ugly Witch,*
Joan. *Son of a Bitch,*
Both. *Would you were hang'd or drown'd in a Ditch.*

        [Here they Dance again.

Pun. *Since we hate, like People in Vogue,*
  Let us call not Bitch and Rogue:
  Gentler Titles let us use,
  Hate each other, but not abuse.
Joan. *Pretty Dear!*
Pun. *Ah! Ma Chere!*
Both. *Joy of my Life and only Care.*

        [Dance and *Exeunt.*

Mast. Gentlemen, the next is *Charon* and a Poet; they are disputing about an Affair pretty common with Poets——Going off without paying.

   Enter Charon *and a* Poet.

Char. Never tell me Sir, I expect my Fare——I wonder what Trade these Authors drive in the other World: I would with as good a will see a Soldier a-board my Boat. A tatter'd Red-coat, and a tatter'd Black one have bilk'd me so often, that I am resolv'd never to take either of them up again——unless I am paid before-hand.

Poet. What a wretched thing it is to be Poor—— My Body lay a Fortnight in the other World before it was Buried.——And this Fellow has kept my Spirit a Month, sunning himself on the other side the River,
           because

becaufe my Pockets were empty——Wilt thou be fo
kind as to fhew me the Way to the Court of *Non-*
fenfe.

Char. Ha, ha, ha! the Court of *Nonfenfe*! why pray
Sir, what have you to do there? thefe Rags look more
like the Drefs of one of *Apollo's* People, than of *Non-*
fenfe's.

Poet. Why Fellow, didft thou never carry Rags to
Nonfenfe?

Char. Truly Sir, I cannot fay but I have, but it is
a long time ago, I affure you; if you are really bound
thither, I'll fet your Name down in my Pocket-Book,
and I don't queftion your Honour's Payment—— *Non-*
fenfe is the beft Deity to me in the Shades——Look at
that Account, Sir.

Poet. [*Reads.*] Spirits imported for the Goddefs of
Nonfenfe, fince *October,* in the Year———— Five People
of great Quality———— Seven ordinary Courtiers————
Nineteen Attorneys—— Eleven Counfellors—— Twenty
fix Juftices of the Peace; and one hundred Presbite-
rian Parfons—— Thefe Courtiers and People of Quality
pay fwingingly, I fuppofe.

Char. Not always; I have wafted over many a Spirit
in a Lac'd Coat, who has been forc'd to leave it with
me.

Maft. Gentlemen, the next is one of *Charon's* Men
with a Prifoner.

Enter Sailor, *and a* Sexton.

Char. How now?

Sail. We have caught the Rogue at laft—— This is
Mr. *Robgrave* the Sexton, who has plundered fo many
Spirits.

Char. Are you come at laft, Sir? what have you to
fay for your felf——ha! what's become of all the Jewels
and other valuable Things you have ftolen? where are
they, Sirrah, ha!

Sex.

Sex. Alack-a-day, I am an unfortunate poor Rogue; the Church-Wardens and Clerks have had them all, I had only a small Reward for stealing them.

Char. Then you shall have another Reward here, Sir. Carry him before Justice *Minos* immediately —— Away with him. 　　　　　[*Ex.* Sailor *and* Sexton.

Poet. Who knows whether this Rogue has not Robb'd me too. —— I forgot to look in upon my Body before I came away.

Char. Had you any thing of Value buried with you?

Poet. Things of Inestimable Value; six Folio's of my own Works.

Mast. Most Poets of this Age will have their Works buried with them.

Enter Sailor.

Sail. There is a great Number of Passengers arriv'd from *England,* all bound to the Court of *Nonsense.*

Char. Some Plague I suppose, or a fresh Cargo of Physicians come to Town from the Universities —— Or perhaps a War broke out.

Sail. No, no! these are all Authors, and a War never sends any of them hither.

Mast. Now, Gentlemen, I shall produce such a Sett of Figures as I may defy all *Europe,* except our own Play-houses, to equal —— Come, put away.

Enter Don Tragedio, *Sir* Farcical Comick, *Dr.* Orator, Signior Opera, Mounsieur Pantomine, *and Mrs.* Novell.

Poet Ha! *Don Tragedio,* your most obedient Servant. Sir *Farcical*—Dr *Orator,* I am heartily glad to see you —— Dear *Signior Opera* —— *Mounsieur Pantomine* —— Mrs. *Novell* in the Shades too! what lucky Distemper can have sent so much good Company hither?

Trag A Tragedy occasioned me to die; That perishing the first day, so did I.

　　　　　　　　　　　　　Farc

Farc. An Entertainment fent me out of the World.
—— My Life went out in a Hifs — Stap my Breath.

AIR IV. *Silvia,* my Deareft.

Oper.   *Claps univerfal,*
      Applaufes refounding;
      Hiffes confounding
      Attending my Song:
      My Senfes drowned,
      And I fell down Dead;
      Whilft I was Singing, Ding, dang, dong.

Poet. Well *Mounfieur Pantomine,* how came you by
your Fate?
Pantom. [*Makes Signs to his Neck.*]
Poet. Broke his Neck: Alas poor Gentleman! ——
And you Madam *Novell?*
Nov. Mine was a hard Cafe indeed.

AIR V. 'Twas when the Seas were roaring.

  Oh! Pity all a Maiden,
    Condemn'd hard Fates to prove;
  I rather would have laid-in,
    Then thus have dy'd for Love!
  'Twas hard t' encounter Death a,
    Before the Bridal Bed;
  Ah! would I had kept my Breath a,
    And loft my Maiden-head.

Poet. Poor Lady!
Maft. 'Twas a hard Fate indeed, in this Age.
Char. Well, my Mafters, I wifh you well. I muft
take leave of you. If you follow that Path you'll
arrive at the Court of *Nonfenfe.*   [*Exit* Charon.
  Poet. Gentlemen, if you pleafe I'll fhew you the
Way.
                           [*Exeunt.*
                              Maft.

Maſt. The next, Gentlemen, is a Blackamore Lady, who comes to preſent you with a Saraband and Caſtanets.　　　　　　　　　　　　　　　[*A Dance.*

Maſt. Now, Gentlemen and Ladies, I ſhall produce a Bookſeller who is the prime Miniſter of *Nonſenſe,* and the Poet.

　　　　　Enter Bookſeller, *and* Poet.

Poet. 'Tis ſtrange, 'tis wondrous ſtrange!

Book. And yet 'tis true — Did you obſerve her Eyes?

Poet. Her Ears rather, for there ſhe took the Infection. She ſaw the *Signior*'s Viſage in his Voice.

Book. Did you not mark, how ſhe melted when he Sung?

Poet. I ſaw her like another *Dido* ——— I ſaw her Heart riſe up to her Eyes, and drop down again to her Ears.

Book. That a Woman of ſo much Senſe as the Goddeſs of *Nonſenſe,* ſhould be taken thus at firſt Sight! I have ſerv'd her faithfully theſe thirty Years as a Bookſeller in the upper World, and never knew her guilty of one Folly before.

Poet. Nay certainly, Mr. *Curry,* you know as much of her, as any Man.

Book. I think I ought, I am ſure I have made as large Oblations to her, as all *Warwick-Lane* and *Pater-Noſter-Row.*

Poet. But is ſhe, this Night, to be married to *Signior Opera?*

Book. This is to be the Bridal Night ——— Well, this will be the ſtrangeſt Thing that has hapned in the Shades, ſince the Rape of *Proſerpine* ——— But now I think on't, what News bring you from the other World?

Poet. Why Affairs go much in the ſame Road there as when you were alive, Authors ſtarve and Bookſellers grow fat, *Grub-Street* harbours as many Pirats as ever *Algiers* did ——— They have more Theatres than are at

Paris, and juſt as much Wit as there is at *Am-ſterdam*; they have ranſack'd all *Italy* for Singers, and all *France* for Dancers.

Book. And all Hell for Conjurers.

Poet. My Lord-Mayor has ſhorten'd the Time of *Bartholomew* Fair in *Smithfield*, and ſo they are re-ſolv'd to keep it all the Year round at the other End of the Town.

Book. I find Matters go ſwimmingly; but I fancy I am wanted; if you pleaſe, Sir, I will ſhew you the way.

Poet. Sir, I follow you.   [*Exeunt.*

Enter Joan, *Lady* King-call, *Mrs.* Glaſs-ring, *and*
Mrs. Cheat-em.

Joan I ask Leave.

All. With you, Madam.

Joan Clubs, and the King of Hearts.

Glaſs. Sure never was any thing ſo provoking as this; you always put me out of a great Game.

[*They play.*

Lady King There's your King, Madam; you have call'd very luckily this Time.——— *Spadille*, there's *Baſto*; we have won our Game.

Joan. I ſay nothing.

King. I'll play it.

Glaſs Then you have loſt it; there is the beſt Dia-mond.

Joan. Was ever ſuch Play ſeen? I wou'd not play with Lady *King-call*, for Farthings.

King I have ſeen your Ladyſhip make greater Mi-ſtakes.

Joan. I wiſh you'd name when, Madam.

King I have not ſo good a Memory, Madam.

Joan. I am ſorry for it, Madam, for you ſeem to want one; it might be of uſe to you.

King

King. I wish you had a better, Madam, it might be of use to Others.

Joan. What do you mean, Madam?

King. I mean, that you owe me a Guinea.

Joan. I believe, Madam, you forget you owe me two.

King. Madam, I deny it.

Joan. And I deny yours.

Glass.
Cheat. } Oh fye, Ladies!

King. It's happy for your Enemies, that your Lady-ship's Character is so well known.

Joan. It would become any body to say so, better than you.——I never stole China.

King. You are an impudent Sow.

Joan. You are an old ugly Sow, and I'll make you know it   [*They fight.*

Enter Punch.

Punch. Have I caught you, Madam? I'll put an End to your *Quadrille,* I am resolv'd. —— Get you home, Strumpet. And you are the fine Ladies who bring her to this —— I'll drive all of you.

　　　　[*Kicks them out, and over-turns the Table.*

Mast. Very uncivilly done, truly, Master *Punch.*

Punch. Uncivilly! why, Sir, since this Game of *Quadrille* has been in Fashion, she has never look'd af-ter my Family; she does nothing but Eat, Drink, Sleep, Dress, and play at *Quadrille.*

A I R VI   To you Fair Ladies.

To all you Husbands, and you Wives,
　　This Punchinello *sings;*
For Reformation of your Lives,
　　This good Advice he brings;
That if you would avoid all Ill,
You shou'd leave off the dear Quadrille.

　　　　　　　　　　　　　　　　N

No Tyrant on the Earth, his Slaves
  With greater Terrour awes;
With Force more absolute behaves,
  Nor gives severer Laws;
Unequal tho' his Taxes fall,
They're with a Smile receiv'd by all.

How many Beauties, rich in Charms,
  Are subject to his Will!
The Bride, when in the Bridegroom's Arms,
  Still thinks on dear Quadrille:
Her Spouse her Body may enroll,
Quadrille *is Master of her Soul.*

The China *People (Sailors say)*
  When they have lost their Pence,
Their Family and Selves will play;
  Heav'n keep that Custom hence!
For Beauties of the first Degree,
May so be Slaves to some Marquis.   [Exit Punch.

Mast. Gentlemen, the next Figures are *Some-body*
and *No-body*, who come to present you with a Dance.

Enter Some-body, *and* No-body.

They Dance.

A I R VII.   Black Joke.

Some. Of all the Men in London *Town,*
    Or Knaves, or Fools, in Coat, or Gown
      The Representative am I:
No. *Go thro' the World, and you will find,*
    In all the Classes of Human-kind,
      Many a jolly No-body.

For him, a No-body, sure we may call,
Who during his Life does nothing at all,
But Eat, and Snore,
And Drink, and Roar,
From Whore to the Tavern, from Tavern to Whore,
With a lac'd Coat, and that is all.

Maſt. Gentlemen, this is the End of the firſt Interlude.

Maſt. Now, Gentlemen, I ſhall preſent you with the moſt glorious Scene that has ever appear'd on the Stage; it is *The Court of Nonſenſe.* Play away, ſoft Muſick, and draw up the Curtain.

The Curtain drawn up to Soft Muſick, diſcovers the Goddeſs of Nonſenſe *on a Throne; the Orator, in a Tub;* Tragedio, *&c. attending.*

Nonſ. Let all my Votaries prepare
To celebrate this joyful Day.
Maſt. Gentlemen, obſerve what a Lover of *Recitativo,* Nonſenſe is.
Nonſ. Monſieur *Pantomine!* you are welcome.
Pant. [*Cuts a Caper.*]
Nonſ. Alas, poor Gentleman! he is modeſt; you may ſpeak; no Words offend, that have no Wit in them.
Maſt. Why, Madam *Nonſenſe,* don't you know that Monſieur *Pantomine* is dumb?——and yet, let me tell you, he has been of great Service to you,——he is the only One of your Votaries that ſets People aſleep

D 4   with-

without Talking. But here's *Don Tragedio* will make Noife enough.

Trag. Yes, *Tragedio* is indeed my Name,
Long fince recorded in the Rolls of Fame,
At *Lincolns-Inn,* and eke at *Drury-Lane.*
Let everlafting Thunder found my Praife,
And forked Light'ning in my Scutcheon blaze;
To *Shakefpear, Johnfon, Dryden, Lee,* or *Rowe,*
I not a Line, no, not a Thought, do owe.
Me, for my Novelty, let all adore,
For, as I wrote, none ever wrote before.

Nonf. Thou art doubly welcome, welcome.

Trag. That Welcome, yes, that Welcome is my Due,
Two Tragedies I wrote, and wrote for you;
And, had not Hiffes, Hiffes me difmay'd,
By this, I'd writ Two-fcore, Two-fcore, by Jay'd

Maft. By Jay'd! ay, that's another Excellence of the Don's; he does not only glean up all the Bad Words of other Authors, but makes new Bad Words of his own.

Sir Farc. Nay, i'gad, I have made New Words, and fpoil'd Old ones too, if you talk of that; I have made Foreigners break *English,* and Englifhmen break *Latin.*———I have as great a Confufion of Languages in my Play, as was at the Building of *Babel.*

Maft. And fo much the more extraordinary, becaufe the Author underftands no Language at all.

Sir Farc. No Language at all!———Stap my Vitals.

Maft. But, Sir *Farcical,* I hear you had once an Intention to introduce a Set of Marrow-bones and Cleavers upon the Stage.

Sir Farc. 'Tis true: And I did produce one Bone, but it ftuck fo confoundedly in the Stomach of the Audience, that I was obliged to drop the Project.

Nonf. Dr. *Orator,* I have heard of you.

Orat.

Orat. Ay, and you might have heard me too, I bawl'd loud enough, I'm sure.

Mast. She might have heard you——But if she had understood your Advertisements, I will believe *Nonsense* to have more Understanding than *Apollo.*

Orat. Have understood me, Sir! what has Understanding to do? My Hearers would be diverted, and they are so,——which could not be, if Understanding were necessary, —— because very few of them have any.

Nonf. You've all deserv'd my hearty Thanks, —— but here my Treasure I bestow.   [*To Signior* Opera.

A I R VIII. Lillibolera.

Op. Let the foolish Philosopher strive in his Cell,
    By Wisdom, or Virtue, to merit true Praise;
The Soldier in Hardship and Danger still dwell,
    That Glory and Honour may crown his last Days;
        The Patriot sweat,
        To be thought Great;
Or Beauty all Day at the Looking-glass toil;
        That popular Voices
        May ring their Applauses,
While a Breath is the only Reward of their Coil.

But would you a wise Man to Action incite,
    Be Riches propos'd the Reward of his Pain,
In Riches is center'd all Humane Delight;
    No Joy is on Earth, but what Gold can obtain.
        If Women, Wine,
        Or Grandeur fine,
Be most your Delight, all these Riches can;
        Would you have Men to flatter?
        To be Rich is the Matter;
When you cry he is Rich, you cry a Great Man.

Nonf. [Repeating in an Ecstacy.]

When you cry he is Rich, you cry a Great Man.
                                        Bravis-

Bravissimo! I long to be your Wife.

Novel. If all my Romances ever pleas'd the Ear of my Goddess —— if I ever found Favour in her Sight —— oh, do not rob me thus!

Nonf. What means my Daughter?

Novel. Alas, he is my Husband!

Curry. But tho' he were your Husband in the other World, Death solves that Tye, and he is at Liberty now to take another; and I never knew any one Instance of a Husband here, who would take the same Wife again.

AIR IX. Whilst I gaze on *Cloe* trembling,

Novel. May all Maids from me take Warning,
  How a Lover's Arms they fly :
Left the first kind Offer scorning,
  They, without a Second, dye.

How unhappy is my Passion!
  How tormenting is my Pain!
If you thwart my Inclination,
  Let me die for Love again.

Curry. Again! What, did you die for Love of your Husband?

Novel. He knows he ought to have been so. —— He swore he would be so. —— Yes, he knows I dy'd for Love, for I dy'd in Child-bed.

Orat. Why, Madam, did you not tell me all the Road hither, that you was a Virgin?

AIR X. Highland Laddy.

I was told, in my Life,
  Death, for ever,
  Did dissever
Men from ev'ry mortal Strife,
And that greatest Plague, a Wife.

For had the Priests poffeſt Mer,
  That to Tartarus
  Wives came after us,
Their Devil wou'd be a Jeſt then,
And our Devil a Wife.

Nonſ. Avaunt, polluted Wretch! begone;
Think not I'll take Pollution to my Arms,
No, no,—— no, no,—— no, no, no.

Oper. Well, ſince I can't have a Goddeſs, I'll e'en
prove a Man of Honour.—— I was always in love with
thee, my Angel.

Novel. Now I am happy, verily.
Oper. My long-loſt Dear!
Novel. My new-found Bud!

AIR XI. Duſty Millar.

Will my charming Creature
  Once again receive me?
Tho' I prov'd a Traytor,
  Will ſhe ſtill believe me?
I will well repay thee,
  For paſt Faults of Roving,
Nor ſhall any Day be
  Without Proofs of Loving.

On that tender lilly Breaſt
  Whileſt I lye panting,
Both together bleſt,
  Both with Tranſports fainting.
Sure no Human Hearts
  Were ever ſo delighted!
Death, which others parts,
  Hath our Souls united.

AIR

AIR XII.　Over the Hills and far away.

Op.　*Were I laid on* Scotland's *Coast,*
　And in my Arms embrac'd my Dear,
　Let Scrubado do its most,
　I would know no Grief or Fear.

Nov.　*Were we cast on* Ireland's *Soil,*
　There confin'd in Bogs to dwell,
　For thee Potatoes I would boil,
　No Irish *Spouse shou'd feast so well.*

Op.　*And tho' we scrubb'd it all the Day,*
Nov.　*We'd kiss, and hug the Night away;*
Op.　Scotch *and* Irish *both shou'd say,*
Both.　*Oh, how blest! how blest are they!*

Orat. Since my Goddess is disengag'd from one Lover, may the humblest, yet not the least diligent of her Servants, hope she wou'd smile on him?

Mast. Master *Orator,* you had best try to charm the Goddess with an Oration.

Orat. The History of a Fiddle and a Fiddlestick is going to be held forth.

A Fiddle is a Statesman: why? Because it's hollow. A Fiddlestick is a Drunkard. why? Because it loves Ros'ning.

Mast. Gentlemen, observe how he ballances his Hands; his Left hand is the Fiddle, and his Right hand is the Fiddlestick.

Orat. A Fiddle is like a Beau's-Nose, because the Bridge is often down; a Fiddlestick is like a Mountebank, because it plays upon a Crowd. —— A Fiddle is like a Stockjobber's Tongue, because it sounds different Notes; and a Fiddlestick is like a Stockjobber's Whig, because it has a great deal of Horsehair in it.

Maſt. And your Oration is like your ſelf; becauſe it has a great deal of Nonſenſe in it.

Nonſ. In vain you try to Charm my Ears, unleſs by Muſick.

Orat. Have at you then.

Maſt. Gentlemen, obſerve how the Doctor ſings in his Tub — here are no Wires ——— all alive, alive, ho!

Orat. Chimes of the Times, to the Tune of *Moll Pately*.

AIR XIII. *Moll Pately.*

All Men are Birds by Nature, Sir,
Tho' they have not Wings to fly ;
On Earth a Soldier's a Creature, Sir,
Much reſembling a Kite in the Sky ;
 The Phyſician is a Fowl, Sir,
 Whom moſt Men call an Owl, Sir,
  Who by his Hooting,
  Hooting, hooting,
  Hooting, hooting,
  Hooting, hooting,
Tells us that Death is nigh.

The Uſurer is a Swallow, Sir,
 That can ſwallow Gold by the Jorum ;
A Woodcock is Squire Shallow, *Sir* ;
 And a Gooſe is oft of the Quorum :
 The Gameſter is a Rook, Sir ;
 The Lawyer, with his Coke, *Sir,*
  Is but a Raven,
  Croaking, croaking,
  Croaking, croaking,
  Croaking, Croaking,
After the ready Rhinorum.

Young Virgins are ſcarce as Rails, Sir ;
 Plenty as Batts the Night-walkers go ;
Soft Italians *are Nightingales, Sir,*
 And a Cock-Sparrow mimicks a Beau :

Like

Like Birds Men are to be Caught, Sir,
Like Birds Men are to be Bought, Sir :
Men of a Side,
Like Birds of a Feather,
Will flock together,
Will flock together,
Both Sexes like Birds will —— *too.*

Nonf. 'Tis all in vain.

Trag. Is *Nonfenfe* of me then forgetful grown,
And muft the Signior be prefer'd alone?
Is it for this, for this, ye Gods! that I
Have in one Scene made fome Folks laugh, fome cry?
For this does my low bluft'ring Language creep,
At once to wake you, and to make you fleep?

Sir Far. And fo all my Puns, and Quibbles, and Co-
nundrums are quite forgotten, ftap my Vitals; but
furely your Goddefsfhip will remember a certain thing
call'd *a Paftoral.*

Or. More Chimes of the Times, to the Tune of
Rogues, Rogues, Rogues.

A I R XIV. There was a jovial Beggar.

The Stone that all things turns at will
To Gold, the Chymift craves ;
But Gold, without the Chymift's Skill,
Turns all Men into Knaves.
For a Cheating they will go, &c.

The Merchant wou'd the Courtier cheat,
When on his Goods he lays
Too high a Price —— *but faith he's bit,*
For a Courtier never pays.
For a Cheating they will go, &c.

The Lawyer, with a Face demure,
Hangs him who fteals your Pelf ;
Becaufe the good Man can endure
No Robber but himfelf.
For a Cheating, &c.

Betwixt

Betwixt the *Quack* and *Highwayman*
   What *Difference* can there be?
Tho' this with *Pistol*, that with *Pen*,
   Both kill you for a *Fee*.
        For a Cheating, &c

The *Husband* cheats his loving *Wife*,
   And to a *Mistress* goes,
While she at home, to ease her *Life*,
   Carouses with the *Beaus.*
        For a Cheating, &c.

The *Tenant* doth the *Steward* nick,
   (So low this *Art* we find,)
The *Steward* doth his *Lordship* trick,
   My *Lord* tricks all *Mankind.*
        For a Cheating, &c.

One *Sect* there are to whose fair *Lot*
   No cheating *Arts* do fall,
And those are *Parsons* call'd, God wot ;
   And so I cheat you all.
        For a Cheating, &c.

Enter Charon.

Char. An't please your Majesty, there is an odd sort of a Man o' t'other side the Water says he's recommended to you by some People of Quality. —— Agad I don't care to take him aboard, not **I**, — he says his Name his *Hurloborumbo* — *rumbo* — *Hurloborumbolo,* **I** think he calls himself, he looks like one of *Apollo's* People in my Opinion, he seems to me mad enough to be a real Poet.

Nonf. Take him aboard.

Char. I had forgot to tell your Ladyship, I hear rare News, they say you are to be declared Goddess of Wit.

Curry. That's no News, Mr. *Charon.*

Char. Well, I'll take *Hurloborumbo* abroad.

                    [*Exit* Charon.

Orat. I must win the Goddess before he arrives, or else I shall lose her for ever. —— A Rap at the Times.

                           A I R

AIR XV.   When I was a Dame of Honour.

Come all who've heard my Cushion beat,
  Confess me as full of Dulness
As any Egg is full of Meat,
  Or full Moon is of Fullness;
Let the Justice and his Clerk both own,
  Than theirs my Dulness greater;
And tell how I've harangu'd the Town,
  When I was a bold Orator.

The Lawyer wrangling at the Bar,
  While the Reverend Bench is dozing,
The Scribler in a Pamphlet War,
  Or Grubstreet Bard composing;
The trudging Quack in Scarlet Cloak,
  Or Coffee-house Politick Prater;
Can none come up to what I have spoke,
  When I was a bold Orator.

The well-bred Courtier telling Lies,
  Or Levée Hunter believing;
The vain Coquet that rolls her Eyes,
  More empty Fops deceiving;
The Parson of dissenting Gang,
  Or flattering Dedicator,
Could none of them like me Harangue,
  When I was a bold Orator.

Enter Punch.

Punch. You, you, you.
Mast. What's the matter, *Punch?*
Punch. Who is that?
Mast. That's an Orator, Master *Punch.*
Punch. An Orator —— What's that?

Maſt. Why an Orator is, is agad I can't tell what; he is a Man that no body dares diſpute with.

Punch Say you ſo, I'll be with him preſently.——— Bring out my Tub there ——— I'll diſpute with you, I'll warrant —— I am a *Muggletonian.*

Orat. I am not.

Punch. Then you are not of my Opinion.

Orat. Sirrah, I know that you and your whole Tribe would be the Death of me; but I am reſolved to proceed to confute you as I have done hitherto, and as long as I have Breath you ſhall hear me, and I hope I have Breath enough to blow you all out of the World.

Punch. If Noiſe will.

Orat Sir, I ———

Punch Hear me, Sir.

Nonſ. Hear him — hear him —— hear him.

AIR XVI. Hey *Barnaby*, take it for Warning.

Punch   *No Tricks ſhall ſave your Bacon,*
         Orator, Orator, *you are miſtaken;*
         Punch *will not be thus Confuted,*
         Bring forth your Reaſons or you are Nonſuited,
             Heigh ho.
         No Tricks ſhall ſave your Bacon,
         Orator, Orator, *you are miſtaken.*

Orat.   *Inſtead of Reaſons advancing,*
         Let the Diſpute be concluded by dancing.
                 Ti, to   [*They dance.*

Nonſ. 'Tis all in vain: A Virgin I will live; and oh great Signior pr'ythee take this Chaplet, and ſtill wear it for my ſake.

Trag. And does great *Nonſenſe* then at length determine
     To give the Chaplet to that Singing Vermin?

Nonſ. I do.

Trag. Then *Opera* come on, and let us try,
     Whether ſhall wear the Chaplet, you or I.

AIR XVII. Be kind and love.

Nov. *Oh, spare to take his precious Life away ;*
So sweet a Voice must sure your Passion lay :
Oh hear his gentle Murmurs first, and then,
If you can kill him, I will cry Amen.

Trag. Since but a Song you ask, a Song I'll hear ;
But tell him, that last Song, is his last Prayer.

AIR XVIII.

Op.   *Barbarous cruel Man,*
I'll Sing thus while I'm dying, I'm dying like a Swan,
I'm dying like a Swan,
A Swan,
A Swan,
With my Face all pale and wan.
More fierce art thou than Pyrates,
Than Pyrates,
Whom the Syrens Musick charms,
Alarms,
Disarms ;
More fierce than Men on the high Roads,
On the high - - - - - Roads,
On the high - - - - - Roads.
More fierce than Men on the high Roads,
Whom Polly Peachum *warms.*
The Devil
Was made civil,
By Orpheus *tuneful Charms ;*
And ca - - - - - -
- - - - - - - - n,
He gentler prove than Man?

Trag. I cannot do it——   [*Sheaths his Sword.*
Methinks I feel my Flesh congeal'd to Bone,
And know not when I'm Flesh and Blood or Stone.
Pant. [*Runs several times round the Stage.*]
                                        Nons.

Nonf. Alas, what means Monfieur *Pantomine?*

Curry. By his pointing to his Head, I fuppofe he would have the Chaplet.

Nonf. Pretty Youth!

Nov. Oh, my dear, how fhall I exprefs the Trouble of my Soul?

Op. If there be Sympathy in Love, I'm fure I felt it —— for I was in a damnable Fright too.

Nov. Give me a Bufs then.

AIR XIX.   Under the Greenwood Tree.

> *In vain a Thoufand Heroes and Kings,*
> > *Should Court me to their Arms,*
> *In vain fhould give me a Thoufand fine Things,*
> > *For thee I'd referve my Charms:*
> *On that dear Breaft, intranc'd in Joys,*
> > *Oh, let me ever be.*

Op.   *Oh, how I will kifs thee,*
> *How I'll emblifs thee,*
> *When thou art a-bed with me.*

Nonf. [*repeats.*] *Oh, how I will kifs thee,* &c.

Sir Farc. Since nothing but a Song will do, I will have my Song too.

Maft. Gentlemen, pray obferve and take notice how Sir *Farcical's* Song fets *Nonfenfe* afleep.

AIR XX.   Hunt the Squirrel.

> *Can my Goddefs then forget*
> > Paraphonalia,
> > Paraphonalia?
> *Can fhe the Crown on another Head fet,*
> > *Than of her* Paraphonalia?
> > *If that had not done too,*
> > *Remember my Bone too,*
> *My Bone, my Bone, my Bone:*
> *Sure my Goddefs never can*
> > *Forget my Marrowbone.*

                     Cur.

Cur. *Nonsense* is asleep.

Trag. Oh, ye immortal Powers!

Sir Far. If any thing can wake her 'tis a Dance.

Omnes. A Dance—a Dance——a Dance.

Enter Charon.

Mast. How now, *Charon?* you are not to enter yet.

Char. To enter, Sir! Alack-a-day! we are all un-done· here is a Constable, and Mr. *Murder-text* the Presbyterian Parson, coming in.

Enter Murder-text *and* Constable.

Const. Are you the Master of the Puppet-Show?

Mast Yes, Sir.

Const. Then you must along with me, Sir; I have a Warrant for you, Sir.

Mast For what?

Murd For abusing *Nonsense*, Sirrah.

Const. People of Quality are not to have their Di-versions libel'd at this Rate.

Murd. No, Sirrah; nor the Saints are not be a-bus'd neither.

Mast Of what do you accuse me, Gentlemen?

Murd. Verily I smell a great deal of A —— bomina-tion and Prophaness——a Smell of Brimstone offendeth my Nostrils, a Puppet-Show is the Devil's-house, and I will burn it —— shall you abuse *Nonsense*, when the whole Town supports it?

Mast. Pox on't, had this Fellow staid a few Mo-ments longer——till the Dance had been over, I had been easy. Hark you, Mr. *Constable*, shall I only beg your Patience for one Dance, and then I'll wait on you?

Murd Sirrah, don't try to corrupt the Magistrate with thy Bribes —— here shall be no Dancing——

verily

verily it is a Prophane Myftery, and hath in it a fuperfluity of Abomination.

Nov. What does this Fellow of a Conftable mean by interrupting our Play?

AIR XXI. Fair *Dorinda.*

Oh Mr. Conftable,
   Drunken Rafcal,
Would I had thee at the Rofe.
   May'ft thou be beaten,
   Hang'd up and eaten,
May'ft thou be eaten, eaten,
    Eaten, eaten,
   Eaten by the Carrion Crows.
The Filth that lies in Common Shores,
   May it ever lie in thy Nofe,
    May it ever
    Lie in thy Nofe,
Oh may it lie in thy Nofe.

Maft. Mollifie yourfelf, Madam.

Murd. Verily that is a pretty Creature, it were a Piece of Charity to take her to my felf for a Hand-maid——————— [*Afide.*

Conft. Very pretty, very pretty truly——— If Magiftrates are to be abus'd at this Rate——— the Devil may be a Conftable for me.——— Harkee, Madam, do you know who we are?

Nov. A Rogue, Sir.

Conft. Madam, I'm a Conftable by Day, and a Juftice of Peace by Night.

Nov. That is a Buzzard by Day, and an Owl by Night.

AIR XXII. New-market.

Conft. *Why, Madam, do you give such Words as these*
To a Constable and Justice of Peace?
I fancy you'll better know how to speak,
By that time you've been in Bridewell *a Week;*
    Have beaten good Hemp, and been
        Whipt at a Post;
    I hope you'll repent, when some Skin
        You have lost.
But if this makes you tremble, I'll not be severe;
Come down a good Guinea, and you shall be clear.

Nov. Oh, Mr. *Murder-text,* you, I am sure, are the
Commander in this Enterprize. If you will prevent
the Rest of our Show, let me beg you will permit the
Dance.

AIR XXIII. Charming *Betty.*

Gentle Preacher,
Non-con Teacher,
Pr'ythee let us take a Dance;
    Leave your Canting,
    Zealous Ranting,
Come and shake a merry Haunch;
    Motions firing,
    Sounds inspiring,
We are led to softer Joys;
    Where in Trances,
    Each Soul dances,
Musick then seems only Noise.

Murd. Verily, I am conquer'd—— Pity prevaileth
over Severity, and the Flesh hath subdued the Spirit—— I feel a Motion in me, and whether it be
of Grace or no I am not certain—— Pretty Maid, I
                                                    cannot

cannot be deaf any longer to your Prayers, I will abide the performing a Dance, and will my self, being thereto mov'd by an inward working, accompany you therein, taking for my Partner that reverend Gentleman.

Maſt. Then ſtrike up.

Enter Witmore, *Mrs.* Moneywood, Harriot *and* Bantomite.

Harr. My dear *Harry!*

Wit. Long live his Majeſty of *Bantam.*

Mrs. Money. Heaven preſerve him.

Bant. Your gracious Father, Sir, greets you well.

Luck. or Maſt. What, in the Devil's Name, is the Meaning of this?

Bant. I find he is intirely ignorant of his Father.

Wit Ay, Sir, it is very common in this Country for a Man not to know his Father.

Luck. What do you mean?

Bant. His Features are much alter'd.

Luck. Sir, I ſhall alter your Features, if you proceed.

Bant. Give me leave to explain my ſelf. I was your Tutor in your earlieſt Years, ſent by your Father, his preſent Majeſty *Francis* IV. King of *Bantam*, to ſhew you the World. We arriv'd at *London*, when one Day among other Frolicks our Ship's Crew ſhooting the Bridge, the Boat over-ſet, and of all our Company, I and your Royal Self were only ſav'd by ſwimming into *Billingſgate*; but tho' I ſav'd my Life, I loſt for ſome time my Senſes, and you, as I then fear'd, for ever. When I recover'd, after a long fruitleſs Search for my Royal Maſter, I ſet Sail for *Bantam*, but was driven by the Winds on far diſtant Coaſts, and wander'd ſeveral Years, till at laſt I arriv'd once more at *Bantam*,—— Gueſs how I was receiv'd—— The King order'd me to be impriſon'd for Life: At laſt, ſome lucky Chance brought thither a Merchant, who offer'd this Jewel as a Preſent to the King of *Bantam*.

Luck.

Luck. Ha! it is the same which was tied upon my Arm, which by good Luck I preserv'd from every other Accident, till want of Money forc'd me to pawn it.

Bant. The Merchant being strictly examin'd, said he had it of a Pawn-broker, upon which I was immediately dispatch'd to *England*, and the Merchant kept close Prisoner till my Return, then to be punish'd with Death, or rewarded with the Government of an Island.

Luck. Know then, that at that Time when you lost your Senses, I also lost mine. I was taken up half dead by a Waterman, and convey'd to his Wife, who sold Oysters, by whose Assistance I recover'd. But the Waters of the *Thames*, like those of *Lethe*, had caus'd an entire Oblivion of my former Fortune——But now it breaks in like Light upon me, and I begin to recollect it all. Is not your Name *Gonsalvo?*

Bant. It is.

Luck. Oh, my *Gonsalvo!*
Bant. Oh, my dearest Lord!   *[Embrace.*

Luck. But say by what lucky Accident you discover'd me.

Bant. I did intend to have advertis'd you in the *Evening Post*, with a Reward; but being directed by the Merchant to the Pawn-broker, I was accidentally there enquiring after you, when your Boy brought your Nab. (Oh, sad Remembrance, that the Son of a King should pawn a Hat!) The Woman told me, that was the Boy that pawn'd the Jewel, and of him I learnt where you lodg'd.

Luck. Prodigious Fortune!   *[A Post-horn without.*

Enter Messenger.

Mess. An Express is arriv'd from *Bantam* with the News of his Majesty's Death.

Bant. Then, Sir, you are King. Long live *Henry* I. King of *Bantam*.

Omnes.

Omnes. Long live *Henry* I. King of *Bantam.*

Luck. Witmore, I now may repay your Generosity.

Wit. Fortune has repaid me, I am sure more than she ow'd, by conferring this Blessing on you.

Luck. My Friend———— But here I am indebted to the golden Goddess, for having given me an Opportunity to aggrandize the Mistress of my Soul, and set her on the Throne of *Bantam;* so once more repeat your Acclamations, Long live *Henry* and *Harriot,* King and Queen of *Bantam,*

Omnes. Huzza!

A I R XXIV. Gently touch the warbling Lire.

Harr. *Let others fondly court a Throne,*
      All my Joy's in you alone;
      Let me find a Crown in you,
      Let me find a Sceptre too,
      Equal in the Court or Grove,
      I am blest, do you but love.

Luck. *Were I not with you to live,*
      Bantam *would no Pleasure give.*
      Happier in some Forest I
      Could upon that Bosom lie.
      I would guard you from all Harms
      While you slept within my Arms.

Harr. *Would an* Alexander *rise,*
      Him I'd view with scornful Eyes.

Luck. *Would* Helen *with thy Charms compare,*
      Her I'd think not half so fair:
      Dearest shalt thou ever be,

Harr. *Thou alone shalt reign in me.*

Const. I hope your Majesty will pardon a poor ignorant Constable: I did not know your Worship, I assure you.

Luck. Pardon you——— Ay more——— You shall be chief Constable of *Bantam,*——— You, Mr. *Murder-text, der-text* shall be my Chaplain; you, Sir, my Orator; you my Poet-Laureat; you my Bookseller; you *Don Tragedio*, Sir *Farcical* and *Signior Opera*, shall entertain the City of *Bantam* with your Performances. Mrs. *Novel*, you shall be a Romance Writer; and to shew my Generosity, *Marplay* and *Sparkish* shall superintend my Theatres———— All proper Servants for the King of *Bantam.*

Money. I always thought he had something more than ordinary in him.

Luck. This Gentlewoman is the Queen's Mother.

Money. For want of a better, Gentlemen.

AIR XXV.   Oh ponder well.

Money. *Alack how alter'd is my Fate!*
What Changes have I seen!
For I, who Lodgings let of late,
Am now again a Queen.
Punch. *And I, who in this Puppet-Show*
Have played Punchenello,
Will now let all the Audience know
I am no common Fellow.

Punch If his Majesty of *Bantam* will give me leave, I can make a Discovery which will be to his Satisfaction. You have chose for a Wife, *Henrietta*, Princess of *Old Brentford.*

Omnes How!

Punch. When the King of *Old Brentford* was expell'd by the King of the *New*, the Queen flew away with her little Daughter, then about two Years old, and was never heard of since   But I sufficiently recollect the Phiz of my Mother, and thus I ask her Blessing

Money Oh, my Son!

Harr Oh, my Brother!

Punch. Oh, my Sister!

Money.

Money. I am forry, in this Pickle, to remember who I am. But alas! too true is all you've faid: Tho' I have been reduced to let Lodgings, I was the Queen of *Brentford*, and this, tho' a Player, is a King's Son.

Enter Joan.

Joan. Then I am a King's Daughter, for this Gentleman is my Husband.

Money. My Daughter!

Harr. ⎱ My Sifter!
Luck ⎰

Punch. My Wife!

Luck. Strike up, Kettle-Drums and Trumpets——
Punch, I will reftore you into your Kingdom at the Expence of my own. I will fend an Exprefs to *Bantam* for my Army.

Punch Brother, I thank you—— And now, if you pleafe, we will celebrate thefe happy Difcoveries with a Dance.

A DANCE.

Luck. Taught by my Fate, let never Bard defpair,
Tho' long he drudge, and feed on *Grub-ftreet* Air:
Since him (at laft) 'tis poffible to fee
As happy and as great a King as me.

4 AP 54

E P I-

EPILOGUE.

1 Poet,	Mr. *Jones*.
2 Poet,	Mr. *Dove*.
3 Poet,	Mr. *Marſhall*.
4 Poet,	Mr. *Wells* jun.
Player,	Miſs *Palms*.
Cat,	Mrs. *Martin*.

Four POETS ſitting at a Table.

1 Po. BRethren, we are aſſembled here, to write
An Epilogue, which muſt be ſpoke To-night.

2 Po. Let the firſt Lines be to the Pit addreſs'd.

3 Po. If Criticks too were mention'd, it were beſt;
With fulſome Flattery, let them be cramm'd,
But if they damn the Play ———

1 Po. ——— ——— ——— Let them be damn'd.

2 Po. Suppoſing therefore, Brother, we ſhou'd lay
Some very great Encomiums on the Play?

3 Po. It cannot be amiſs ———

1 Po. ——— ——— ——— Now mount the Boxes,
Abuſe the Beaus, and Compliment the Doxies.

4 Po. Abuſe the Beaus! ——— But how?

1 Po. ——— ——— ——— Oh! never mind.
In ev'ry modern Epilogue, you'll find
Enough, which we may borrow of that kind.

3 Po. What will the Name of Imitation ſoften?

1 Po. Oh! Sir, you cannot ſay good things too often;
And ſure thoſe Thoughts which in another ſhine,
Become not duller, by becoming mine.

3 Po. I'm ſatisfy'd

1 Po. ——— The Audience is already
Divided into Critick, Beau, and Lady;
Nor Box, nor Pit, nor Gallery, can ſhew
One, who's not Lady, Critick, or a Beau.

3 Po.

EPILOGUE.

3 Po. *It muſt be very difficult to pleaſe*
Fancies ſo odd, ſo oppoſite as theſe.

1 Po. *The Task is not ſo difficult, as put;*
There's one thing pleaſes all.

2 Po. —— *What is that?*

1 Po. ——— *Smut.*
For as a Whore is lik'd, for being tawdry,
So is an Epilogue for ————

3 Po. [in a Paſſion] ———— *I order you,*
On Pain of my Departure, not to chatter,
One Word ſo very ſav'ry of the Creature;
For, by my Pen, might I Parnaſſus ſhare,
I'd not, to gain it all, offend the Fair.

1 Po. *You are too nice* ——— *for ſay whate'er we can,*
Their Modeſty is ſafe behind a Fan.

4 Po. *Well, let us now begin.*

3 Po ———— ——— *But we omit*
An Epilogue's chief Decoration, Wit.

1 Po. *It hath been ſo; but that ſtale Cuſtom's broken;*
Tho' dull to read, 'twill pleaſe you when 'tis ſpoken.

Enter the Author.

Auth *Fie, Gentlemen, the Audience now hath ſtaid*
This half Hour for the Epilogue ———

All Po. ——— ———— ——— *'Tis not made*

Auth. *How!* —— *then I value not your Aid of that,*
I'll have the Epilogue ſpoken by a Cat.
Puſs, Puſs, Puſs, Puſs, Puſs, Puſs, Puſs.

Enter Cat.

1 Po. ———— ——— *I'm in a Rage*
When Cats come on, Poets ſhou'd leave the Stage.
                                    [Exeunt *Poets.*

Cat. *Mew, Mew.*

Auth. ——— *Poor Puſs, come hither pretty Rogue,*
Who knows but you may come to be in Vogue?
Some Ladies like a Cat, and ſome a Dog.

Enter

EPILOGUE.

Enter a Player.

Play. *Cafs! cafs! cafs! cafs! Fie, Mr.* Luckleſs, *what*
     Can you be doing with that filthy Cat? [*Exit* Cat.
Auth. *Oh! curſt Misfortune —— what can I be doing?*
     This Devil's coming in has prov'd my Ruin.
     She's driv'n the Cat and Epilogue away.
Play. *Sure you are mad, and know not what you ſay.*
Auth. *Mad you may call me, Madam; but you'll own,*
     I hope, I am not madder than the Town.
Play. *A Cat to ſpeak an Epilogue ——*
Auth. *———————— ſpeak! — no,*
     Only to act the Epilogue in Dumb-Show.
Play. *Dumb-Show!*
Auth. *—— Why, pray, is that ſo ſtrange a Comedy?*
     And have you not ſeen Perſeus *and* Andromeda?
     Where you may find ſtrange Incidents intended,
     And regular Intrigues begun and ended,
     Tho' not a Word doth from an Actor fall;
     As 'tis polite to ſpeak in Murmurs ſmall,
     Sure, 'tis politer, not to ſpeak at all.
Play. *But who is this? ——*

Enter Cat *as a Woman.*

Auth. *———————— I know her not ——*
Cat. *———————— I that*
     Am now a Woman, lately was a Cat.
               [Turns to the Audience.
     Gallants, you ſeem to think this Transformation
     As ſtrange as was the Rabit's Procreation;
     That 'tis as odd a Cat ſhou'd take the Habit
     Of breeding us, as we ſhou'd breed a Rabit.
     I'll warrant eating one of them wou'd be
     As eaſy to a Beau, as —— kiſſing me.
     I wou'd not for the World that Thing ſhould catch us,
     Cries ſcar'd Sir Plume —— *Fore-gad, my Lord,*
       ſhe'd ſcratch us.

EPILOGUE.

Yet let not that deter you from yo͜u Sport,
You'll find my Nails are par'd exceeding short.
But—Ha!—what Murmurs thro' the Benches roam!
The Husbands cry——we've Cat enough at home.
This Transformation can be strange to no Man,
There's a great Likeness 'twixt a Cat and Woman.

    Chang'd by her Lover's earnest Prayers, we're
       told,
A Cat was, to a beauteous Maid of old.
Cou'd modern Husbands thus the Gods prevail on;
Oh gemini! what Wife wou'd have no Tail on.
Puss wou'd be seen where Madam lately sat,
And ev'ry Lady Townly *be a Cat.*

    Say, all of you, whose Honey-moon is over,
What wou'd you give such Changes to discover;
And waking in the Morn, instead of Bride,
To find poor Puffy purring by your Side.
Say, gentle Husbands, which of you wou'd curse,
And cry, my Wife is alter'd for the worse?

    Shou'd to our Sex the Gods like Justice show,
And at our Pray'rs transform our Husbands too,
Many a Lord, who now his Fellows scorns,
Wou'd then exceed a Cat by nothing—but his **Horns.**
So Plenty then wou'd be those Foes to Rats,
Henly *might prove that all Mankind are Cats.*

F I N I S.

Ingram Content Group UK Ltd.
Milton Keynes UK
UKHW051156180423
420361UK00008B/699

9 781140 683025